A Riot of Thorn and Leaf

By Dulcie M. Matthews

with illustrations by
Brett D. M-Tipper

First published 2001

Hayloft Publishing, Kirkby Stephen, Cumbria, CA17 4EU.
Tel. (017683) 42300 or fax. (017683) 41568
e-mail: dawn@hayloft.org.uk
Web: www.hayloft.org.uk

ISBN 0-9540711-0-7

A catalogue record for this book is available
from the British Library

Cover photograph by Dulcie Matthews

Printed by Lintons Printers, Co. Durham.

...to my son for his love, time & patience. And to <u>all</u> those who have believed in me when I haven't, and to my husband for all his support and help throughout.

Best Wishes
Dulcie M Mathie

A RIOT OF THORN AND LEAF

.....It began with snowdrops growing in the secret corner of a wood -
Windy Scout Brow wood. A love affair that has lasted for ten years,
growing in depth and intensity with each month that has passed. Now I
have gathered together each thought, each timeless moment, to paint a
picture. A tribute to and a celebration of.........my sense of place. Each
month includes diary excerpts from the past ten years, showing clearly
how no month or season is ever predictable.

I am in love.
In love with the wind on silver wing
that flies among the waiting trees.
In love with the laugh of the rushing stream,
caressing stones upon its way.
My heart is wooed with sweet persuasion by the breeze,
Then won with simple pleasure
at the golden dawn of day.
I am in love.
In love with the riot of thorn and leaf
which natures wanton humour twines.
Enamoured by a butterfly as it rests on
the heart of an eager flower.
I breathe with delight the musk perfume
of raindrops falling on the pines.
Then gaze in awe at the flaming sky
which brings to close the days last hour.

January

January has roared in on a gale. The field across the lane has become a lake, whipped into waves by a howling wind blowing in from the sea. From the warm security of my cottage, I can see lapwings, oyster-catchers and seagulls making the most of the water. Trees in Windy Scout Brow Wood bend and sway precariously, and the cats find warm corners of the cottage to curl into. More logs on the fire, a closed curtain, and I am content.

A day of not feeling well has had it's advantages. For a long time I have been able to sit and watch life from my window. A large variety of birds have jostled for the nuts which hang just outside. They form a queue, clinging onto the wall, and sometimes, the window. The flooded field has shone - it's frozen surface reflecting sun. Two small children from the bottom cottage have played on it for most of the day, sliding and pulling each other along on their home-made sledge. Now, at four-o-clock, the setting sun has flooded the ice with deep orange. Four cats have slept most of the day, preferring the log fire to the frost.

The field opposite is now drained of water again, and oyster-catchers have occupied it through-out the night, and again in this morning's sun. Their gentle calls are comforting to hear. They have now been joined by lapwings.

Almost tea time, and the sky is palest translucent blue, gold-streaked, - dark bare trees silhouetted against it making it look like a delicate Chinese porcelain vase.

The fresh wind of yesterday which whispered the promise of Spring to snowdrops, has been replaced by a damp misty day. Blue tits are tapping on my window to remind me to fill up the nut hopper. They have finished up the seed cakes I make with lard - with a little help from the other birds. As I pour nuts into the hopper, they sit in near-by bushes, chattering.

The day began with the loudest thunder-clap I have ever heard. It was swiftly followed by hail storms which left the fields white. Downstairs, four cats were all staring out of the window, eyes huge and tails outstretched. The hail stones had found their way down the chimney, scattering soot everywhere. Who ever heard of thunder storms in January! I heard later that the mighty thunder clap had hit the Crag.

The wind today has made an arch over my gate lean dangerously. A few more gales and it'll be down. Ah well! Daisy has found soot or coal dust in the garden, and looks a disgrace. Out of four cats, it would be the white one who rolled in soot. She is now offended because she was refused my lap.

A fresh day with a lively wind tempted me to the cliffs this morning. Looking across the Bay with its wide sweeping sands is such a pleasure. The tide was coming in quickly, lapping water racing over the sand. The wind was alive, blowing away the old cobwebs - carrying Spring's whispers everywhere. It must have stirred the cats too, as a mad dash by Daisy and Lux left devastation. My special plant on the floor, and soil spilt everywhere! Now, they are curled up in four sleeping balls, the fire is crackling, and all seems so peaceful.

Sun shining on my cottage window today, showed up the salty grime thrown at it by the gales of the past week. Now, it is so still, so I am going to walk to Jack Scout cliffs, along the lane to the Giant's Seat. I pass cows feeding from the byre. It's a comfortable sound, and the sweet-sour smell of the silage is glorious, though my Granddaughter doesn't agree with me.

The dog from Tower House Farm walks warily to check me out and then to greet me. He is very appealing - one ear up, one down. The sun casts lazy shadows across my path. Birds are calling to each other - Spring is ever closer, and they know. A tiny wren hops into the hedge, disappearing beneath vibrant green tongue ferns. Walking home, I become fascinated by the ancient grey crumbling walls. Ivy spills over them, old gnarled tree roots spill and scramble through their crevice's. Last year's brambles tangle into the roots. Rich green moss covers the stones, and a heavy wooden gate hides amongst the ivy. The latch is rusted, and looks as though it hasn't been opened for centuries. Maybe it's the 'Secret Garden'. The last stretch now before home, and a pause to watch lapwings wheeling arcs across the Dyke.

I have stood today and watched snow falling, softly, gently, relent-lessly. It has blown in dense white flurries from Jenny Brown's Point, across the fields, around my cottage - to settle on the earth, cover the new shoots prematurely showing. I have again filled the nut hopper, and hardly closed the door before birds queued to feed. The cats have sat and watched through the cat flap and the window. They seemed mesmerised by this endless falling white curtain. Lux, the most curious of the four, ventured out to chase snow flakes, and was joined by Daisy, who didn't look so white against the snow! They were soon in again, glistening with crystals which melted into little pools on the floor. Now, it's a fight to gain space by the log fire - and I am losing!

A clear and sunny day; walking across the Dyke to the Giant's Seat, I stepped on small pools to hear the ice crack. Two curlews dipped and dived across the field, calling to each other, - the heron made his slow deliberate flight along the stream. Flying low, he suddenly rose, resting on the air currents - magnificent. The tide was rushing in; no leisurely lapping this, but energetic white horses galloping to the rocks. It was a high tide, already reaching the wall of Jenny Brown's cottages - push-ing up the ice in small pools and causing movement beneath their sur-face. The smell of vegetation mingled with seaweed. The rocks were slippery, and as usual - I managed to fall.

It was a wild, wild night. Trees bent to touch earth, battered by the howling wind. Plastic carrier bags swirled in the air like enormous white birds before settling on fences and wrapping themselves around branch-es. Birds seem to have given up completely. Tired of riding on winds that have no direction. The lane was littered with twigs, branches. Some of the smaller trees, long since dead, now blew along the lane like match-sticks. Down came my TV aerial, joining the arch which became a casualty of yesterday's blasts. Logs on the fire blazed away cheerfully - ignoring the angry gusts trying to reach them down the chimney.

Today arrived quietly, wearing grey veils. Sky, field, sea - all varying shades of the same colour. The world was still and waiting. The nut hopper hanging outside my cottage window brought great fun, adding colour to a drab new world. Blue tits flocked to feed, clinging on to the pebble-dashed wall. The bird table was another source of pleasure. Robins guarded it aggressively, trying in vain to copy the tits hanging upside down approach. Bullfinches and chaffinches fed in unconcerned manner, ignoring the bad manners of the robins. The woodpecker arrived, pecked holes in the mesh nut hopper, and then turned his attentions to the bird table stand. Because of his attacks on the mesh hopper, I have now added a metal one. The good side effect of holes in the mesh bag has been the sparrows and starlings, who, always quick to seize an opportunity, have eaten the fallen nuts. No doubt small shrews and mice will tidy up the remainder during the night. In nature, nothing is wasted.

The daily comings and goings of the birds are always supervised by my four cats, who sit on the windowsill to watch. As they are confined to house and back cat garden, the birds are safe. They seem to know, and often peer in at the window, which makes it an absorbing and harmless occupation.

After a day that began grey and remained leaden - at tea time the sky made breath catch in my throat. Bands of turquoise, duck egg blue, laced together with iridescent flaming orange. Black-grey clouds drifted across the colours, the sea flooding blood red as it mirrored the sky above it. Birds still singing made it sound like Spring. It is very mild - 50 degrees fahrenheit.

There I was, stumbling about in the undergrowth, dry twigs cracking beneath my feet, last years brambles tangling in my hair, and the wood becoming denser with every step. Panic was replaced by laughter as I ended up for the third time passing the same fallen tree. The grikes were moss covered; deer droppings lay in secret places by the edges of an ancient tumbling wall. Sunshine reached delicately to the darkest places, lighting up tongue ferns and the green carpet of Spring to come. Sunny fingers stretched through the sleeping tangle of growth. Snowdrops huddled in cosy clumps by grey rocks. Birds singing Spring songs belied the month. I followed Beau my Labrador blindly until we found the path where arum lily was growing, and passed a field alive with dancing snowdrops. Now I knew where I was! I passed the time of day with

JANUARY

Charlie the farmer's horse, then headed for home.

Incredible gales! For two days and nights the winds have torn like wild banshees across the fields, everything bending in their path. Greyness has been swept away, the apathy of the years beginning now replaced by the urgency of the gales. Skies are blue, sun painting colour onto field and sea. The copper shades of Leighton Moss bird reserve glowing against green and blue. Birds struggle in the blasts, then give in and rest themselves on the wind. Last year's leaves live for a second time as they do a Dervish dance, swirling around in a lively frenzy.

Today was very cold; icy wind hurling hail stones at my cottage windows and coating the fields in white lace.

Snow blizzards during the night still lay on the fields this morning, sparkling in the sun. Hail showers blew across the Jack Scout cliffs on their way to rap at my windows. They made rainbows against the sun. Snowdrops danced defiantly, small green-edged cups raised hopefully to the sunlight. So many snowdrops - a snowdrop year.

Will this wind never go? Gales of 90 miles per hour today blew snow in its destructive blast. The air became alive with swirling ice. The Dyke flooded onto fields; dark days indeed. An old man in tattered inadequate coat bent into the wind, struggling to hold on to his carrier bags. Where would he sleep or find shelter? How did he become a lost soul, with all his world in three bags? So many unanswerable questions.

This morning the gales had gone, as mysteriously as they had arrived. Bright sun rested on the hills. Such a contrast following the wildness of the past few days. The adagio movement following the agitated allegro. Walking through and beyond Beetham village, I clambered over the gales legacy - trees fallen in grotesque shapes. Amazingly, snowdrops still bobbed cheerfully in white drifts. How do they survive? My walk took me past an old derelict cottage and on through a wood where sugary snow was sprinkled across the path - crystallised onto leaves and branches. The air was clear and still. On to the fields where I watched a tractor, the steady sound of its engine carrying clearly in the sharp thin air. Smoke from chimneys of distant cottages rose in swirling grey spirals into a blue blue sky. Walking homewards, two grey squirrels darted across the lane, pausing, whiskers twitching, before their swift retreat into the trees.

The frost was still here; pristine, diamond white, it covered the fields, sparkling many faceted in the sun. I walked through the reed beds at the

Bird Reserve, watching cold winter sun curl frail skeletal fingers round naked trees. Pale gold reeds bent gracefully beneath their frosting. Such stillness! The sky, pink-tinged made the sea around Jenny Browns Point glow. Back home to a welcome log fire, I watched the busy activities on the bird table. A hen blackbird has taken the table over, refusing to let other birds feed. Even the robin has given in to her. The birds seem to feed in shifts. The nut cakes I make from nuts, seeds and lard are very popular.

The sun is becoming kinder. It has turned from the icy cool aloof and reluctant, into a more friendly gold. Its arrow beams touching distant hills and grey rocks. Today, there is a breeze making snowdrops bob excitedly, their dance joined by green-yellow catkins and new born lambs. This is a day of life and beginnings, as the countryside feels the stirring of Spring. Primrose nestles against crocus. This year they are flowering early, in time to join the snowdrops dance to Winter.

Today I walked from Silverdale village to the Cove; such a clear day. I headed across the fields. Ahead, lay the Bay, distant and still. The tide had retreated leaving behind hollows of shining pools. Pieces of jig-saw waiting to be re-assembled by the next incoming tide. I reached the cove and clambered up to a deep cave in the rocks, where I found a pound coin left behind by a previous visitor. Such a stillness around me - a hopeful expectance. On to Eaves wood accompanied by bird song. Snowdrops were in abundance, having defiantly faced January's snow and winds. Not today though - today it was damp and moist. A smell of vegetation and wood fires. Moisture hung in silver droplets on the branches. I kicked my feet through last year's leaves. Verdant ferns curled in hidden places. The trees blushed slightly, showing early signs of life. Returning to the cottage, a flock of greylag geese flew noisily overhead. Flying very high, silhouetted against a sinking sun.

Such an incredible sight this evening. Dusk was prematurely black, with starlings coming in to roost. They filled the sky as they descended in an endless stream, so that the tree seemed impossibly inadequate to hold them. Their high pitched twittering rose above the wind. Still they came - noisily plummeting, on the back of the wind.

Outside my cottage tonight, the world was silent. Darkness held fields in a strong suspended moment. Flooded fields shone softly silver as the moon admired her reflection. Owls' calls carried across empty spaces, echoing, answering. Tonight, the newly made lake had tempted other birds, piercing the night-black with wistful notes. Clear and melancholy.

I wondered which bird made such sounds, feeling angry at my lack of knowledge. But maybe the name doesn't matter - the haunting beauty of its call was still the same.

Fields have become lakes, as constant rain has fallen for days. Water washed down from Warton Crag spills over the lane and onto the fields. Last year's leaves, once gold-amber, now lie on the garden and in the wood in sodden colourless dejection. Through the grey stillness, were woven threads of green and silver - fields benefiting from rain - pools of water reflecting morning light. Waiting trees stretch bare branches, raindrops hang in shining rows.

The sky is full of rain; it has fallen constantly all day, and now evening has merged into afternoon, subtly blending night-dark with wet-grey. The cats have wandered in and out disconsolately - trying first one door and then another, just in case the weather is different. Maui has brought us in a worm. She presents it with pride, holding it so gently that it remains intact, to be returned to the garden. During Autumn she brings us leaves, but it's always worms in the Winter.

Today, the wind was fresh. A pale shadowy sun slipped elusively behind wisps of cobweb grey cloud. A blue-streaked sky reflected in the sea. I walked into Silverdale via Jenny Brown's Point, reaching the lane just in time, as the tide was coming in. Sea poured steadily, resolutely, at a fast pace, helped along by the wind. No sign yet of white violets - they still sleep beneath hedges, waiting for a warmer sun. Returning over Heald Brow, I stopped to look around me. From here I could see the shining stretch of the Bay, flat salt marshes, and the grey bulk of Warton Crag with my cottage sitting securely in its shadow. Curlews' calls carried far on the wind. Stopping again, I watched the greylag geese fly in noisy ragged formation to feed on the edges of the marsh.

After the rain of the past few days, the hopeful brightness this morning was very welcome. The daily chores become a pleasure. A walk in the wood with the dog was a good start. Rain had shone the ferns and decorated the branches - which are now beginning to show off new buds. I walked back across the lawn very carefully so that I didn't tread on daffodils' new shoots. Next, the cleaning out of ashes in order to get a log fire going. This is the minus side of living flames. It's a chore that is unpopular on wet days and cold or windy mornings. Today, it was a pleasure. The cats, full of energy after being house-bound for days, thought this was yet another game devised by me for their entertainment. The mixture of ash and mud on numerous paws was not a pleasure!

There are no more fallen and dead trees, so I took a trip to Arnside to buy logs from a local farm. Together with a friend, we walked along the shore at Sandside to watch seagulls wheeling in the wind and oyster-catchers wading along the edge of a receding tide. Getting the log sacks out of the car was a Laurel and Hardy routine. We struggled up the uneven cottage path - and dropped the sacks thankfully against the locked gate of the cat garden. I then went through the house to move the sacks, because, guess what, we couldn't open the gate from the inside because we had leaned the sack on it!

It had rained all day. The cats did their usual check to see whether it was the same at all doors, then settled sulkily by the fire. These grey days are a wonderful reason for a fire, and good too for catching up on odd jobs. The dog and I did have a wander through the wood before tea time, and enjoyed the huge soft snowflakes that replaced the rain. Strong winds still blowing whirled the flakes into frantic eddies, but wet ground didn't encourage them to settle.

Grey mists of endless rain cling sadly to the hills today - draping downwards onto fields now deep in water. Two herons, wings out-stretched, legs down, flew silently overhead. A prehistoric landscape - timeless, washed in mystery. Warton sat at the crags' foot, surrounded by water; a grey-stone island. Lambs rested close to their mothers for shelter. So early to be born into this cold wet world.

February

February has entered the year shyly, wearing smoky grey. Sky and sea merged together. Snow has fallen softly - lightly, sprinkling field and hedgerow, turning to slush on the lane. Overhead, the greylag geese were on their noisy journey to the Bird Reserve. Plaintive curlew cries pierced the speckled mist.

I awoke this morning to a still, white world where grey stone walls and leafless trees stood out in stark contrast. How changed was the landscape. By noon, an orange sun had melted away the whiteness and turned the sky to a delicate flush of peach. It seems that most of England is battling with an excess of snow, yet here in this little corner of north Lancashire we have only white frost and wintry sunshine, thanks to the protection of sea and surrounding hills of the Lakes. Twin lambs lay, tiny and helpless on the frozen field. Golden catkins dusted with silver hung in the hedges.

The month progresses - it has become mild and sunny, and birds are busy mating. Garden and wood alike beginning to stir with new life.

Back to damp mist this morning - the air is very still as if waiting. My much loved grey cat Chloe has not come home today.

Drizzly, grey and shrouded - a forgotten day. Fields and trees draped sadly in mist, patiently waiting for spring. Chloe has not yet returned; where is she, this small cat as grey as the mist that hides the wood, as lithe as the movements of shadows? I walked into the silent wood calling her name. A rustle as the grass moved, but it was just an illusion. Nothing else stirred on the damp woodland path. Branches cried silent tears on my head as I passed; all was still.

Today was much brighter. The mist had lifted and the woodpecker has begun his special drumming in the wood. By afternoon it was quite warm. How exciting to see the aforesaid woodpecker sitting on my bird table tucking into my especially made seed and lard cakes. The snowdrops have shaken off raindrops, and raised hopeful faces, showing their delicate green edged frills. No greeting today as I come into my room in the morning. No soft grey cat with owl-like eyes and a demanding meow. One more search in the wood and a final pause to remember last week when I laughed as she ran up a tree in one swift dash, then turned and asked to be lifted down! Now I will accept her going and be glad for the three years of fun and pleasure she gave so gladly. (A small note here - Chloe disappeared in 1992, and a cat garden is now in place to protect my cat family.)

My walk today felt sad. A slight movement around my feet, a fleeting shadow. Maybe Chloe saying her farewells.

February is such a fickle month. As I awake this morning to another still, white world, the sounds of the day are muffled - silent anticipation everywhere. The wood has become new, its bare floor now covered in a virginal white carpet. Trees dripping with crystals bowed beneath the weight. Hills, snow-capped, tinted palest peach in the early morning sun. Birds are busy examining nesting sites. In the secret corners of Windy Scout Brow Wood, snowdrops hide, but become braver as I approach the field. Here, they reach out eagerly from beneath the hedges. Dainty wild daffodils are now pushing through dead undergrowth, and peering from curling tongue ferns.

This afternoon I walked to the Fairy Steps at Beetham; such a gentle stillness here. Sun smiled on the snowy carpet, lighting up golden beech leaves and old ferns. Hidden beechnuts crunched beneath my feet. Long graceful catkins, green-yellow, bobbed cheerfully. I trod carefully over slippery rocks and hidden grikes. The path was becoming muddy as a warmer sun melted snow.

The woodpecker was back on my bird table again this morning - such an honour! A walk in the awakening wood accompanied by dog and cats to find Spring seemed in order. It is lurking in the forming buds, betrayed in bird song, revealed in the woodpeckers rhythmic drumming. Snowdrops nod heads to each other from their leafy beds. They can hear spring.

Cold sun shone today. It touched the sea, then slid like pale gold silk around my shoulders, draped itself around the clouds. I was encased in a cocoon of sunlight, yet I was cold. No warmth yet; it lit up winter's dirt on my cottage windows! I set to and began cleaning them, feeling like a mass murderer. It took so long to re-house the spiders into the shed, that the job took twice as long. Wiping away their intricate cobweb homes felt like an act of desecration.

As the frosts and mists have chased each other, the fields have become flooded. A fresh blustery day is now blowing ripples across the surface of an instant lake where fields had been. Water birds have quickly discovered it and the whole lake is teeming with life. The woodpecker has returned yet again to swing to and fro on the bird feeder. He looks somehow incongruous. During the night the wind gained strength, throwing itself angrily at my cottage. It shook windows, and tore at the foundations until it seemed that the cottage would be wrenched free and tossed into the wood beyond. I awoke to an even bigger lake, whipped into a frenzy by the wind. Swans and seagulls had taken up residence. Sun shone on its surface - but - serenity was short-lived. As I watched, I could see rain approaching in a swirling grey cloud. It reached the cottage, hurling spiteful spikes of water at the windows. February can be a very bad tempered month!

Angry gales have again torn around the cottage all night. In fury they have ripped trees free by their roots, scattering them with the unconcern of a litter lout across the lane. The daffodils lay beaten and dejected on wet grass. Delicate flowers, tempted out by a fickle sun, now face spiteful spears of rain spiked with ice. Snowflakes sharp and cold, ride on the wind's back, hurling themselves at my face.

A walk in the wood in a sunny interval between blasts shows my wood living up to its name of Windy Scout Brow! The gale's capricious frolics have left a trail of broken branches. As usual, my companions were dog, and today, just two cats. An instant and unwelcome hailstorm made me take cover, sheltering the smallest cat in my coat. The path became suddenly white as small stinging stones pelted down. The dog and remaining cat were back at the cottage door before me today! The lake is now even bigger - wind whipping up waves across its surface. Curlew, black capped gulls, swans, didn't seem to mind. Snow has again fallen heavily, but melted into grey wetness on contact with the ground.

The wind was still blowing this morning as I set out for Jack Scout cliffs. I sat awhile watching the stormy racing sea, seagulls resting on the wind. It tore around me as I clambered across rocks, going upwards as the tide was licking around the cliff bottom.

This afternoon was calmer, so I walked out to examine gale and flood damage. A tree lay across the lane, a wounded giant fallen victim to a delinquent wind. Tight new buds still unborn, clung to each branch, unaware that the source of life lay severed at its base. Still surviving on the sap flowing through the tree. It looked clumsy lying there, and I cried for its passing.

After endless days, at last, a warm sunny spring day that was so very welcome. Snowdrops have been replaced by primroses and violets. I walked up to Warton Crag and looked down at the village and fields below. Shimmering silver, islands surrounded by floodwater. As I stood on the Crag's edge, a butterfly settled! How incredible - so early. Such a fragile life to weather gale and flood. A final look at my instant lake that now boasted swans, cygnets, gulls, geese and a solitary heron, then home to a crackling fire and hot tea.

The oyster-catchers made such a frenzied whistling sound this morning. They have moved onto the flooded field, which is wonderful, as I wake and sleep to their sounds.

Another damp wet day promises to keep the field nicely topped up. Now, tonight, their whistles have become gentle comforting coos, with occasional conversational calls. I drifted into sleep listening.

St. Valentine's Day; the oyster-catchers flew in a graceful arc, curving against a soft apricot-white sky. Flying in perfect symmetry as a single body, they disappeared towards the sea, so the tide must be in.

I went quietly through the wood, as if walking through the room of a sleeping friend. Nothing moved; tall naked trees stood still, no gales today. Dead colourless leaves lay in soggy profusion - a blanket to cover sleeping plants.

A lively wind woke up the day and made the cats frisky. Sultan brought in a tiny wood shrew. It was alive, wriggling in his mouth. He was so surprised, he dropped it at my feet and before I could pick it up to return it to the wood, it ran for safety - into a hole in the skirting board under my stairs! Sultan, assisted by Daisy and two others, kept watch over the hole for ages, with no luck. I hope the shrew manages to find his wood again.

The world it seems, is awash with water. It falls from heavy clouds, flows in streams down the lanes, floods the fields. Rivers swell and spill over, bloated with water. Sheep press against walls and hedges as rain becomes sleet, stinging and relentless. They look bedraggled, their lambs huddling close for soggy protection. Only the sea birds find pleasure. Oystercatchers call in ecstatic whistles, ducks, lapwings, all feeling that their wet world is perfection. Which just shows that you can't please everybody.

England is a land of contrasts. Its moods change from day to day and are never boring. Today, fresh winds blow ripples creating a moving world of splintered sunlight on yesterday's water - and lifts birds heaven-wards. Sun touches the ripples and coaxes out reluctant buds. It is a day for life - for feeling new life awakening.

Simkin is spending a little precious time in his favourite pastime - watching the washing machine throw clothes around. He sits engrossed until it stops, and nothing will distract him

A warm gentle day: I sat on the bench with the cats and watched the birds being busy. Daffodils are beginning to grow strongly. Primroses open shyly and snuggle up to violets. Trees, still bare, are beginning a whisper that soon will become a shout, though just now, the whisper is only faintly green. The wood is slowly stretching and waking up again.

A walk to Jenny Brown's Point today. I stood awhile to wonder at the power and beauty of a swan as it flew overhead, its wings making a steady beating sound. The mesh fence on the shore at Jenny Brown's Point was wearing a green lace curtain of seaweed - the legacy of a high tide. Lapwings swooped and dived as they mastered and used the playful wind. Their haunting cries echoing across the empty spaces. Sullen grey clouds hung sulkily above a grey sea, moving reluctantly with the wind. Mingled sounds sang a magic duet. Twisted tree trunks along the lane stood unbending, their skeletal branches still waiting for new spring clothes. Silhouetted against the sky they became enchanted. This was a strange magical land. Silvery sun rays reflected on the sea as it moved swiftly inland again whispering its breathless sighs, stretching ever in, wrapping around waiting rocks. The sun became braver, pushing back the still pouting storm clouds.

17

This evening I watched the sun set from my window. A flaming golden orb, it admired its beauty in the mirror of the sea before slipping quietly away, pulling grey night clouds over its head.

Once again I was tempted by a seductive sun to go to Jack Scout cliffs when I should have been doing other things. A cold night had iced the pools of trapped water, which were then polished to a glassy sheen by the morning sun. They crunched deliciously under my feet. Celandines are out, just a few. Soon they will be followed by the less brave arums. Rich dark shining green leaves are already uncurling in the hedgerows. I watched a small bird disappear into a hole in an ancient tree. Though I waited awhile, he didn't oblige me by popping out so that he could be identified. Walking back over Heald Brow, the morning had a breathless clarity. Feathery snowflakes floated downwards, swirling around me as light as dandelion thistledown - brushing my face softly before resting on the grass and disappearing.

The dog and I walked across the fields today in a snowstorm. The snow swirled about me but didn't settle on the hard ground. Each snow shower was followed by sunbursts, as if the sun was playing a game with the snowflakes. Though we found it exhilarating, the dog trying hard to catch the flakes, sheep were pressed against the wall for shelter. The stream that usually bounces happily over stones, was today - still - suspended in a frozen moment, held captive by ice. In the distance, sun highlighted the snow topped Lakeland hills. Despite the cold and the snow, Spring is sleeping, waiting to stretch and bring new life. It isn't far away!

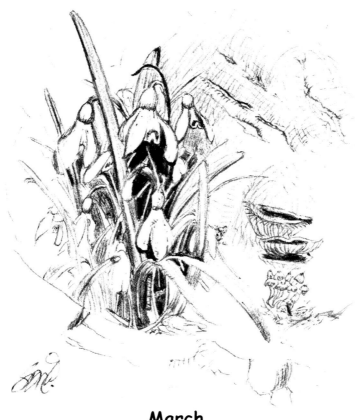

March

Following folklore, March duly came in roaring. The first weeks brought snow, hail storms and gales that tossed garden benches about like match-sticks. Seeking out the bedroom chimney, the wind moaned all night long, changing to a sobbing sigh as the gales eased.

After a cold night and late Spring frost, the sun shone. I walked in Levens Park with the unaccustomed feel of sun on my back. There was ice on the river, and along the river bank, icicles hung in a shining curtain; an impressive Cathedral organ. I was watched closely as I walked over gently swelling grassland, by a herd of deer. Sunbeams searched for the river, poking arrow beams through the trees. On finding it, they splintered into a myriad sparkling dancing patterns on its surface. Beech nuts mingled with Autumn's old overcoat, crunching beneath my feet. The deer, tiring of disturbance, moved silently together and crossed the river.

For the past week, the unpredictable English weather has been wet. A March which began with sunny promise has changed its mind again. There has been a week of grey mornings - sea and sky merging into dismal drizzly dampness. Then - with the speed of a sigh, came windy days, bending the newly budding daffodils and howling across open fields. My jeans clung desperately to the clothes line, almost going to Jenny Brown's Point without me inside them! All night the wind had roared around the cottage trying to get in. It crept under doors, rattled locks, and breathed impatiently down the chimney.

Walking to Silverdale village today, I was bewitched, watching the long grass rippling, billowing as it bowed to the wind. A vast green sea afloat with sheep.

This confused March weather gives each day a magical variety of surprises. Sun, rain, wind, create skies painted in fluorescent colours. Peach-blushed clouds hover over the sea - rain hanging in grey lace curtains beneath them. The shore has become white with seagulls feeding in noisy querulous groups. They swoop and dive, performing amazing aerial feats. The sky has now become black with starlings coming in to roost. Evening sun, deep gold, now stretching lazily, reaching out from clouds which were turning to grey cotton-wool, resting onto a sea still aflame with sun-gold.

Sun this morning gently tiptoed over the hills, rested on the sea, then gaining confidence, reached inwards touching fields and hedges - waking up sleeping violets and primroses. Hedgerows now have a pale green mist settling across them as new shoots rush to greet the sun. What had begun as a whisper, was becoming a shout of Spring. The air was warm; it became heavy with bird song. Sheep, maternal, watched over their lambs, who oblivious to anything beyond the moment, ran, jumped and nestled into their mothers' woolly warmth. Maybe they have the answer to living, by enjoying the very moment they occupy. No past to regret, no future to anticipate.

Showers today spoke more of April than of March. All day the sun chased showery clouds, causing them to weep onto the fields. Now this evening I am held captive, as an iridescent curtain of light floods onto the sea, field and lane. The sky has become sullen and heavy, as a perfect rainbow arches magnificently. A complete bow resting on the sea, pouring its pot of gold onto the grass.

The earth is becoming warmer, so today seemed a good time to work in the garden. Last year's dead growth was hampering the new, and the garden was calling for help. Using the fork was hazardous, as the cats were quite convinced this was a new game thought up just for their enjoyment. They dived at the fork, chasing the flying debris. Sultan was definitely not amused when I showered him with soil. As they were all insisting on helping me dig, it was difficult to avoid them. I pushed the wheel-barrow loaded with dead growth and two cats. Sheldon followed at a safe distance - which was all fine until the contents were tipped onto the compost heap. Now three cats sat washing nonchalantly as they gained lost dignity. Cleo sat on the shed roof watching. Older and wiser than the others, her look showed contempt as she examined her claws.

This Spring sunshine has stirred other things as well as my garden. A rustle in the bathroom fern revealed a tiny pipistrelle bat that had some- how got himself stuck inside. My loft is home to these delightful little creatures. He came to rest on the cistern pipe, his wings tightly wrapped around it. Looking a million years old, he eyed me warily from a tiny wizened face. I removed him gently, releasing him into the night air - but not before he had bitten the hand that saved him.

Tiny wild daffodils are flowering in the wood - deep gold celandines glow in the hedges and along my garden path. They have chosen to keep company with the aubretia, and I haven't the heart to remove them. A large yellow butterfly flies in glorious bursts - the afternoon sun is pale and reflective. The world is coming alive in many shades of gold.

I woke up to the sight of lapwings, swirling arcs over the field, sun turning their wings to silver. The flooded field is alive with birds. The sun's fingers became more insistent, lifting the last edges of morning mist. Walking on the cliff tops, all was still and crystal clear. I trod gen- tly through green grass sprinkled with small shining rainbows. The clump of white violets that had warily lifted their heads a week ago, were now boldly looking outwards, with rainbow droplets around their shoul- ders.

A curtain of hailstones bounced to the earth, in such a frenzied hurry to reach their destination they bounced erratically onto the ground and threw themselves at the windows. Then, as suddenly as they came, they stopped. A nervous sun peeped out, anxiously searching out the places left white by the hailstones, touching them gently with warm fingers, melting them to small pools.

A RIOT OF THORN AND LEAF

Snow fell tonight, just when Winter seemed to be bending before Spring. It came silently, in soft white powdery swirls - mesmerising me as I drove along the lane. A moving vortex, drawing me inwards. Walking in the garden, my face was delicately caressed. Flakes clung to hair and eyebrows.

Snow lay on rumpled hills this morning. A white blanket on an unmade bed. Clouds of creamy pearl and smoky agate parted to allow the sun to gently touch the earth.

There was such a commotion this evening in the kitchen. Time to settle down, lock out the cold night and sit by a log fire, sharing it with four cats and one dog. How wrong can you be! The cats refused to leave the kitchen, but sat, ears back, crouching motionless by the cupboard. I could hear scurrying - not another wood shrew! They creep in unseen, then get stuck behind the kitchen cupboards. Suicidal shrews! Nothing would coax the cats away. Sadly, in the morning - one dead shrew lay on the floor; such lovely little things.

The new couch arrived this morning. It has been sniffed, stalked, walked round and watched for hours. Now it has become a new claw sharpening post, despite my shouts. At last, it has been approved of, and two cats are asleep on it, one in each corner.

I awoke this morning to a sunny world sprinkled liberally with white icing sugar. Grass wore frost like a powdered wig. The cats were both puzzled and delighted - running in and out in swift bursts, ears back and tails at odd angles. Two hens scratching in my garden (visitors) were having difficulties because of the hard ground.

Things are warming up at last. A walk along the lane this morning was wonderful. First day without a coat - the air soft and warm. Pools left by a receding tide were flooded blue by the sky. Bluebells have begun to push their glossy spikes through winter weary earth. Warton rested at the foot of the Crag looking safe and ageless, its Church tower presiding. The graveyard holds safely the graves of the Washington family. On my way back, a car driving too fast and with no thought for wild life, hit a crow. How sad on such a lovely Spring day to see him suddenly lifeless - eyes now vacant, staring at a sky he cannot see. Glossy black feathers still reflecting the sun.

A walk to Woodwell in warm sunshine. The well was alive - a seething mass of frogs coming back again to mate. Their guttural croaking as they hopped and dived among the reeds, filled the air with rhythmic throbbing sounds. Frog spawn on the surface of the water was an assuring sign of a thriving frog population. A symphony on double bass accompanied by the flute songs of birds.

Sitting on the Giants seat, I gazed out across the shining sands. An ebbing tide was leaving patterns and many shades of colour on the sands. All was still and timeless - water seeping into the shifting sands breaking the silence. Gulls called, curlews cried, as they searched the still wet sand for food.

The softness of the past few days has again been replaced with rain and strong winds which hurl themselves from sea and field to bend new shoots and fragile daffodils with spiteful glee.

A walk around the garden this morning to rescue the daffodils lying forlornly on the grass. It is a capricious side of nature's humour that follows the emergence of delicate flowers with gales of cold wind.

Though still cold and windy, the sun in sheltered places was warm today. I walked with dog and cats through the wood to look for Spring. Wild daffodils are fading, but the scene which greeted me was unexpected - devastation everywhere! Piles of brushwood covered tiny violets and pale primrose as they struggled to grow in their suddenly hostile world. Tree stumps severed, bare trunks bore the Wood's wounds. Deep tractor tyre marks had bitten into the earth with no respect for orchids and bluebells, violet or primrose. They lay torn and scattered in the path of the tractor. Maybe it was coppicing, maybe there is a reason for this carnage - I can only hope. The small Spring flowers will recover to carpet the woodland floor again, new trees will flourish for birds and other wild-life to cover themselves in. Hope and new life are always there, it is just necessary to hope.

The evening sky following a sunny day was a wash of delicate colour, lightly touched with brush strokes - feathery wisps of grey swirling downwards to merge with apricot.

Icy cold blasts mocked sunshine this morning. Sharp hailstones stinging my face, stopped as suddenly as they had begun, leaving white trails across the garden. Hailstones rested in new furling leaves, sparkling in the sun.

Early morning frost lay on the fields and garden to greet my waking. Primroses drooped sadly, but as the sun grew warmer, they once more lifted faces up and smiled. March is ending warmly wistful, and today was almost like early Summer. A walk to Jack Scout cliffs was transformed into magic by the sight of white violets along the lane. Flotsam included a tree trunk that had been moulded by the sea to look like a giant slice of melon.

Today began with a crash. One of the cats had jumped on the window-sill to watch birds, knocking plants off in the process!

As it was a fresh Spring morning, I walked into Warton village over the crag. Tiny purple violets cover the verges. Above me, seagulls swooped, rose, fell, circling and calling. They always sound so cross, their raucous cries echoing around me. Rubbish was an unwelcome reminder of week-end visitors to the crag. A dustbin had been foraged by animals, its contents scattered over the lane. A covered bin might be helpful. Although I had been told that the trees that had edged the lane for so long, needed to be cut down because they damage walls and prevent wild flowers from flourishing - I still find the sight of the bare wounded trunks very distressing. Maybe time will heal their wounds, as it does ours.

A stormy morning; lead-grey clouds hanging low over fields, being chased across the sky by a sharp angry wind blowing in from the sea. New leaves and daffodils bend to let it pass - easier than fighting. Two cats run into the wood in erratic jerky frenzy, running up trees, chasing imaginary mice across the lawn. A game of hide and seek among the daffodils before going in for breakfast

Showers continue to chase sunshine as March nears her end. Catkins and shining silver palm have withstood early winds - the first celandines shine gold on grass verges. Blue tits have taken to clinging on the windows, peering into my sitting room. All around me, Spring yawns and stretches, adorning herself to greet Summer.

Walking through to Silverdale today, I was going to talk to a lovely gentleman of 87 years, whose grandfather began the locally well known Shaw Hadwin firm in 1872. White violets nestled in tree roots, and a very deep purple violet grew in the lane to the village. It had been a sunny day when I set out, but grey clouds stretched across the sun on my return, making the day seem brooding and expectant. I disturbed a goose who had been viewing the lane. He turned, and with a dignified waddle went back into Hazelwood Farm. Some lovely knobbled tree trunks at the edge of the village were shaking hands over a wall.

Now, during its last week, March has become a lamb. Sitting in my cat garden in warm sunshine, I have surveyed with a never fading pleasure the new shoots of plants as they push through the earth. The cats are blissful; they roll on their backs, hide behind daffodil clumps and dive on each other.

Last day of March, and I stood to watch a robin. He sat on the old stone wall, bright red breast on show, eyeing me with curiosity, but no fear. It is a debatable point as to who was watching who! He eventually tired of the waiting game and hopped into the rambling ivy and dead leaves.

Night-time on the last day of March; it feels so good to see soft darkness arriving later. As Spring approaches, the day becomes more reluctant to leave. A blackbird continued to sing his clear, beautiful song as the night gently urged daylight to fade.

April

Iawoke this morning to sunshine shimmering on white frosted fields. The tide was in, water sending blue reflections back to the sky. English April weather, so unpredictable and alive. Various finches and tits vied for place on the nut hopper, their acrobatics spectacular to watch as a sudden unexpected gust of wind made it swing wildly. Within half an hour - all had changed. A swirling grey cloud hid the sun, blew from the sea towards the cottage, and hurled angry hail-stones at my windows. Daffodils lay on the lawn. Once again a capricious Spring had lured them out, only to flatten them.

The new carpet was coming this morning, so with help from my son, we stacked furniture, cushions, ornaments onto one side of the room. This is a tiny cottage, so planning is of paramount importance. Unwittingly, we had created a cats playground. Four cats chased, hid and dived onto each other from new secret places. All very amusing until a delicately balanced couch gave in to pressure and fell, bringing with it cushions, books and small breakables. Four cats scattered to dark corners upstairs, giving the new playground a wide berth.

The day was warm and gentle. Lanes stretched and lay in the sun - trees rested their long shadows across my path creating shade. Two rabbits on a grass verge sat, unconcerned - munching. Even the sheep and young lambs had caught the soporific mood, sleeping on the warm fields, their lambs nestling beside them. A pheasant ran out from the wood, frightened by the sudden noise of a twig as it cracked underfoot. His erratic escape accompanied by raucous complaints at the unexpected disturbance. Such was the feel of this day, that even the greylag geese in the field next to my cottage, were temporarily silent.

A three dimensional sky demanded my attention this morning. White clouds, foamy and light, drifted across the blue back-cloth. Heavy grey clouds scudded past them, occasionally releasing rain onto fields. Crows were busy carrying twigs, their beaks bulging. They expertly rode the breeze. More crows sat on the back of sheep, who didn't mind at all, but carried on grazing. A lone heron flew above me, his prehistoric shape silhouetted against the sky. It was an English sky. The early flush of green set against white and grey clouds floating across each other. I felt I could fall into their fluffy softness - lie in them. Poplars reached upwards, slender spires piercing the clouds. I watched a kestrel hovering, his wings beating furiously. He plummeted suddenly earthwards onto the rich dark newly ploughed field. As the evening sun set, clouds turned to a vivid orange, highlighting a pair of swans, black against the sky. The beating of their wings filling the soft air with rhythmic drumming. White hawthorn blossom shone in the fading light, became snow in the hedges.

Looking like a painting on silk, the hills in many shades of grey melted into a pearl grey sky - sloping and shading ever backwards. It was a gentle, secret, misty morning. The mist slowly cleared to reveal a pale sun. April is being very kind. Now, I sat watching the day slide away. Lazy smoke trails spiralled upwards from the field. The evening sun blushed pink and hid her face behind darkening hills.

It has been a 'cat day'! Sheldon had sat by the bushes for hours, and just when I had forgotten him, he came dashing through the cat flap with a tiny baby rabbit in his mouth. This is when I feel such anger toward them, even though I know he is just obeying ancient instinct. I managed to release the rabbit amidst lots of growling, and took him back to where he came from. Sheldon was grounded for the remainder of the day. (Another small note here; despite a later cat garden to keep them safe, Sheldon managed to get out, and one day, he just didn't come home again. Having known freedom, and being an inveterate wanderer, he became an incredible escapologist, and was impossible to keep confined, even in a big and lovely garden complete with cat frame. This is a wonderful construction of big logs, complete with small platforms, so that they can climb, sit to view, and scratch their claws.)

Confinement meant that four cats were looking for mischief, which they found in the bathroom where a tin of paint had been left with the lid slightly loose. A big part of my day was spent in cleaning paws and carpet!

At tea time, the warm weather became heavy - the sky, scowling. Bands of peach gave way to blue-grey angry clouds and thunder roared, its loud voice sending birds skywards, making the cats sit alert, and even disturbing the dog! Jagged lightning flashes lit up the sky, more thunder shaking the windows and rattling doors.

The following morning was dewy eyed and fresh. Bluebells now cover the woodland floor, blending with green ramsons and dog mercury to turn the wood into a fairy tale. Early sun reached pale fingers through the now dense leaf canopy, transforming raindrops from last night's falls into shining miracles. Droplets rested on leaves, settled into the heart of each flower, and showered onto me as I brushed branches in passing. My walk was accompanied as always by Beau, and today, two cats. Just to be friendly, two cats from next door came too. Aware of the sunny freshness, they chased each other through undergrowth, up trees, emerging wet furred. Birds singing loudly echoed the pleasure of this beautiful morning. The wren was trilling her ecstatic song, its volume out of proportion to her size.

Because I find it so difficult to stay inside, especially when the sun is so warm, I took my papers outside to work. I should have known better. The distractions were numerous. Greylag geese having noisy discussions in the field, the mesmeric hum of insects, birds calling to each other. All glad to be alive in this golden moment, like me. Orange tip butterflies are busy, as are large yellow and cabbage white. The kittens from next door, aided and abetted by Sultan, were doing amazing acrobatics in vain efforts to catch them. The lure of sight and sound was hypnotic, but I forced myself away eventually in order to work. Not for long! Looking from the kitchen window wistfully, I saw a large white rabbit peacefully chewing my plants. Feeling like Alice in Wonderland, I tried to catch him. He disappeared through a hole, but this one was through the hedge back to his own garden - and I didn't follow him.

Though still quite cold, a reluctant sun shone on the white violets now growing in clusters in the lane from Jenny Browns Point. I had a wonderful view of the solitary heron as it flew above me, wings spread wide, feet down, as he rose from the stream. No doubt I had disturbed him as I struggled to carry an oriental looking piece of flotsam (or is it jetsam?)

back home.

After baking all day I went into the wood and fields beyond with the dog and two cats - glad of company. Sun had smiled down all day, and now rested on Leighton Moss, a shining golden mirror. Wild daffodils are fading as ramsons flourish, releasing a pungent smell of garlic as I pass. Violets and primroses fight for space and reach for the sun through dead bracken and fallen trees. Daisy chases bees, Sultan chases Daisy, who runs up trees like a squirrel, her tail twitching magic circles. Back now into the garden where two visiting kittens lie in wait amongst my daffodils. The wren is still singing as if her heart would burst. She must have a nest on the edge of the wood again.

This is a changeable month, sun and showers chasing each other. Today, a leaden sky has been pierced with silver darts of light that have touched the fields. Snow edged distant hills sparkled in arrow beams. On warm days I have sat in the garden watching it come to life. The wren is still singing - hedges have emerged from their hazy green mist into a definite statement of Spring. The woods are now speckled white with hawthorn and crab apple blossom, and celandines have studded the fields with gold. A few violets still linger, though the white violets have now faded. Buttery clumps of cowslips push pale primrose faces aside.

Today, an icy wind blowing from the sea made me shiver. Frost had transformed green into silver in the early morning. Hail storms, spitefully sudden, have rattled at the windows. Lambs run and chase in the fields, happy despite their unpredictable world.

April progresses and has become warm and sunny. Time now to sit outside watching the first orange-tip butterflies rushing from flower to flower. The wood is awash with blue. Bluebells cover the woodland floor, orchids growing amongst them. Primroses and a few violets still jostle for space. The air is heady with the scent of bluebells mingled with wild garlic and the sweet almost antiseptic smell of hawthorn blossom. I walked through the wood, surprising a deer the colour of tree bark. He melted silently into the undergrowth.

Last night's unexpected rain and wind had gone this morning, leaving grass and trees sparkling in the sun. Only the sad confetti blossom petals strewn carelessly on the ground giving evidence of the storms.

An early morning walk to Burton Well and Wood Well. It was misty and mysterious, cobwebs dripping with dew hung precariously between bending reeds. Ladysmock grew in pale pink profusion. Mist hugged the grass and hedges, turning verdant green into deep intense colour. The air smelt 'green'! By Burton Well, marsh marigolds were shining. Streams running under fields and sometimes bubbling forth have made this place a haven for wild flowers. Stitchwort, ladysmock, bluebells, primrose, violet and water avens growing happily together in the marshy meadow. Beau jumped into the stream, emerging as a two-toned Labrador. She shook mud over me, and was not popular. On the rocks above Woodwell I could hear lambs bleating and their mothers anxious replies - just sounds echoing, hidden in a wraith-like mist. The church bells from St. Johns in Silverdale floated across open spaces. Walking on to Jack Scout, I paused to listen to sea birds calling. Their melancholy cries echoing across silent sands. Along the dyke, I stood again to watch lapwings circling. Skylarks, unseen, sang joyfully. The mist was lifting, and though an old saying is that one skylark does not make a Summer, as the mist dispersed it revealed a glorious day.

Hesitant buds have now become bold, bursting into bloom. Baby rabbits bob about everywhere as I walk.

A deer darts across the woodland path - a squirrel scurries and plays among new shoots. Skylarks hover and sing - a Red Admiral butterfly flies erratically, bemused by Spring.

Searching in the potting shed for garden tools, I discovered two butterflies who had chosen my shed to hatch out in. They were tangled in thick cobwebs, and struggling frantically. This time I cheated the spiders and rescued them to fly free. The sun was warm on my back as I took a welcome break from gardening. I sat on the bench looking through a sea of daffodils to the hills and sea beyond. Daisy was chasing a butterfly, and leapt at least three feet in the air in an unsuccessful attempt to catch it. Sultan was rolling on his back dabbing at moving grasses - such a tempting target! Simkins jumped on him from the bench, knocked down the watering can, and made three cats run in opposite directions. Tiring of the game, Simkins stalked through the grass. He hates wet paws, so shook each paw in turn as he walked. He is such a comical little cat, always looking as if he needs to take off his heavy white boots.

I love April - everything is new, fresh. Lambs, goslings, rabbits - they burst with a joy just to be alive. A stormy sky made a wonderful backdrop to banks of primroses. White hawthorn blossom stood out in stark contrast to grey clouds.

Hail stones bounced around my feet, going as suddenly as they had arrived. Butterflies are appearing - Peacock, Chalk Blue Brimstone.

Grass verges have become misted blue with tiny speedwell flowers.

I have walked today on a magic carpet delicately woven in shades of yellow, blue and green. Tiny stitches of violet woven into primrose, oxslip, bluebells, orchids - and I have felt content.

A tortoiseshell butterfly which has wintered in my bedroom has decided to wake up. Sitting in the palm of my hand, we went together into the garden where I sat on the bench watching it. Seemingly weak, it made a sudden bid for freedom, soaring away skywards. These are the things which are important in an uncertain and often cruel world. Each year, these small miracles happen, reinforcing the basic certainty of new life.

May

The first few days of May have been so warm and sunny. Orange-tip butterflies are beginning to increase in numbers, and the woodpecker is sending out his rhythmic messages from the now leafy wood. Speedwells have spread across my lawn - it is a blue and green world. Walking into the shady cool of leafy branches, a shimmer of blue lay in front of me as bluebells began to open.

Still the sun continues! It's eight in the evening and I am watching a lazy sun slide reluctantly into the sea. Insects are still busy, the sound of their buzzing joins the songs of birds - all reluctant to let the day go. My cats emerge from their cool hidden spots to dab, half heartedly at passing butterflies - and to ask for supper.

Lapwings in shimmering flight against a May blue sky, swirled above me - the sun turning them into shooting stars. I walked through my garden to the wood beyond, blossom petals falling around me in soft pink showers. Bluebells have painted the wood in cool colour.

Walking to Jenny Brown's Point, I took time out to watch a tractor ploughing the field. Rich brown earth fell in tidy furrows, seagulls made noisy circles as they followed the tractor's progress. Moments like these give the feeling that just for a moment, the world has stopped, and give a continuity which is comforting. Swallows swooped and soared around me as I crossed the Dyke, the deep iridescent blue of their wings glinting in the sun's light. Sitting on the Giant's seat, the stillness was breathless. An ebbing tide had left behind it vast smooth sweeps of sand, shining curves of colour. Walking homewards, sheep and lambs scattered indignantly before me. One sheep decided to move quickly but with dignity. She walked in front of me - an elegant oversized lady in high heels, stumbling on the rocky shore.

Tapping on the window tonight announced the rather late arrival of the May bugs. Though they can be very disconcerting as they fly clumsily in the evening garden, there is still something re-assuring in their arrival.

A warm day, the sun almost appearing, and a chance to do some work in the garden. Moving a large rockery stone, I discovered an ants' nest, and sat on the grass to watch them for a while before replacing their refuge.

The starlings' nest in the eaves has been busy all day. The poor parents working a continuous shift system to feed a very noisy brood. My cats have gazed up all day, but all in vain, as thankfully, they are safely in their cat garden - and the starlings are not!

The field that spends Winter as a lake, has today had its lush grass mown. The drone of the tractor is a continuous sleepy sound, and the smell is wonderful.

Walking to the shore tonight, sun slid away, blue-black clouds hung over the Bay. They gathered, amassed, gaining strength, moving insidiously towards me. Trees whispered to each other secretly, the message passed from one to another. Anticipation became intense - colours deeper. Sand, clay-brown, water abandoned by a receding tide, bottle-green. Hawthorn blossom heady scented. Then - low rumbling, sinister warnings. The sky rent apart with razor sharp shards of light. The rumble became a roar which touched to the core of my being, as the waiting trees were engulfed with silver rain, sheets of hard water bouncing onto the hard welcoming earth. Walking home, the storm had moved on, leaving soft grey rain behind it. No more whispering trees, there was relief now in lifted branches. The rain had turned grass and leaves into shining vibrant green - the air smelt fresh and new. Ahead of me, mist hung in a sheer film over the field - sheep and lambs appearing suddenly as they headed for shelter beneath trees. My legs, in shorts, were very wet, yet all I felt was exhilaration in this new-washed world.

Arriving back at the cottage, already anticipating hot tea, I was greeted by four wet indignant cats, and a power cut! After feeding and drying the cats (priorities!) I lit all available candles, had a welcome candlelit hot bath, and settled down in the half-light to a wonderful meal of cold all sorts gleaned from fridge and cupboard. The silence is an experience in itself. No radio or cooker noises, just bird song and dripping raindrops.

These first weeks of May have been so sunny and warm. Shafts of sunlight turned green leaves into silver - Orange-tip butterflies weaving their erratic flight from flower to flower, watched and chased unsuccessfully by the cats. Sun has made the cats lazy. They stretch out in the warmth, making occasional desultory moves under bushes.

Early mornings at this time of year are delicate, full of tremulous promise. Pale sun shines leaves still wet from last night's showers. Arums look ghostly, their pale eerie green hoods opaque, luminous, like lanterns in the early light.

A darkening sky this evening made the moon look huge. It hovered over the hills - a Halloween lantern lit to an orange glow from within. The May bugs have arrived exactly on cue. They bang clumsily into the windows. These large flying Cockchafer beetles almost seem to have their wings accidentally, flying with no sense of direction and even less skill.

The sun is still shining. The endless shades of green in leaf and fern mingling with bluebells in the wood look cool and inviting. So far, the showers have fallen in the early mornings, leaving all fresh and new. No wilting woodland or drooping garden yet. Curlews call to each other, and the wren trills loudly from first light to early dark.

Early evening, and still the sun shines, transforming the field and sea into a shimmering mirage. Along the lane a field has been mown, leaving symmetrical lines curving upwards in graceful sweeps, looking like neatly combed hair. The smell of ripe grass is welcome. Reluctant to go indoors, the cats and I sit and watch butterflies and bees making the most of the sun and long evening. Midges buzz around me, heralds of a fine tomorrow. The sky slowly changes from clear blue to peach, aquamarine, flame orange - the sun, from burning gold to deep amber. It too seemed reluctant to let go of this day, slowly sliding into the sea.

The narrow lane had become a heavily perfumed tunnel, each side a dancing mass of cow parsley, campion and bluebell. Walking along it, intoxicated by the scented air, I felt diminished in size. Alice in a wonderland of gently swaying colour.

Late evening, the lane grey-dark. Walking with the dog into a darkness that melted in front of me. Bats flew their darting zigzag flights - fleeting shadows, gone in a moment. Ramsons glowed eerie white - night lanterns to show me the way. The scent of new-mown grass still lingered - the tractor not long finished its long day, now beaten by fading light. Now, the field lay in neat furrows, hidden in night-dark.

Two weeks of warm sun have been replaced amazingly by strong winds and icy rain falls. The treacherous sun has once again tricked flowers into opening, and they now lay across the dark earth dejectedly. New blossoms and leaves have deserted the trees to decorate the lane in green and pink showers. Just thirty miles away the roads lay under four inches of snow! As I walked head down along the lane, I paused to let a small weasel scurry to the hedge in front of me; no doubt looking for some shelter. The cats play their usual wet weather game of going out of one door and calling for admittance at the other. They then complain loudly to me - it's my fault that their favourite places are now wet and cold.

Yesterday and today, the rain has been steady and relentless. A fine grey mist has clung lankly to the fields, painting sky and sea the same colour. Flowers lie dashed and dejected. Pale petals litter the lane - yesterday's confetti. The field opposite, newly mown, now lies under water, where only days ago it basked it sun. No doubt seagulls and swans will soon appear.

The flooded field looked ghostly in the half light of evening. Bats made silent flights above me. So many night sounds made lane and field sound busy. Seagulls had discovered the new 'lake', their argumentative conversations still in progress. Owls joined the chorus as they searched for supper.

The past week has been very changeable. A month that began softly warm has become grey, wet and windy. The garden has opened up its treasures in red, blue, green and yellow, but now lies flattened by spiteful rain and fickle gales blowing from the sea.

This morning the lawn and lane are littered with branches and new leaves, torn off by the wind in its bad temper. The cats made such a fuss about a tiny body on the path. On first sight it appeared to be a small mouse, but on closer scrutiny it was a pipistrelle bat. Still alive, it lay in my hand watching me with ancient eyes in a wizened face. Its tiny mouth opening silently to reveal minute but very sharp teeth. Feeling very inadequate, I hung him on a tree in the wood where the green was dense and dark. Sadly, he didn't survive the day.

Despite the wet weather, there have been no toads this year. I miss seeing them outside my back door, and wonder why they have deserted my cottage. Cobweb, the tiny ball of grey fluff who joined us on 1 May, is growing fast, and delights in jumping on the other cats and the dog. Unimpressed, they spend their time avoiding him. His fresh delight in all new things is a constant pleasure. A whole morning can be spent contemplating and stalking a leaf.

The day was clear, promising - a warm gentle May. It is so good to walk early on these mornings. Wind-flowers are growing amongst the bluebells; Leighton Moss shimmering in the distance.

A few toads have returned once more from their earthy hibernation. I now need to be careful where I step in the evening. They peer at me with their myopic steady gaze. It also means that the grass cannot be cut for a while for fear of hurting them. Pipistrelle bats are again in residence in my loft, though not so many this year.

The wood is in full leaf, wearing her best gown for Spring in many shades of green. May is continuing warm, and as I climbed today over ancient grey rocks known as the 'Fairy Steps', the air was soft on my skin, like a newly washed blanket. The fields lie green in the sun, studded yellow as buttercups lift small faces. Spring is wearing her best perfume. Woodland paths have transformed into glowing colour with wild flowers, and pheasants run awkwardly in front of me giving their raucous alarm cries. Lambs are growing quickly, and now run in little groups further away from their mothers. They jump, run and chase, on and off hayricks and walls. Stopping to watch, two smaller lambs came to say hello. They greeted the dog, and nestled noses into my hand. These two must have been hand reared, and their trusting made me sad.

Ladysmock and stitchwort now grow under hedges, primroses still cluster around the trees, small pale gold faces floating on a green sea.

Violets, aconites, strawberry flowers, cowslips, celandines, daisy, dandelion and daffodils huddle together in cosy confusion. Orange-tip butterflies rush from flower to flower. The mini heat wave has now cooled, and light breezes alternate with sun and showers. The work on the field opposite has continued, and it has now been seeded. I shall await with interest the next stage. It's odd now to remember when it was flooded and home to swans - gulls, yet it was just a few months ago. Now, the birds swoop and cry across its neatly tilled brown surface.

Such a noise and fuss this morning as the sheep were brought along the lane from the Jack Scout fields - probably for dipping. Their indignant bleating made such a din, and also created a tail-back of holiday traffic for miles. There is always so much to watch. The saddest moment is when the lambs disappear and their mothers call for them.

As I drove home at midnight, rain fell. Hard, bouncing rain, hurling itself at the road, sparkling in my headlights. Rabbits ran in front of me, dashing unpredictably from side to side before going through the hedge. A fox on the lane was caught for one second in my lights, before streaking off into the night. Quite an eventful drive home, as two deer suddenly appeared and just as quickly, vanished into the wood. It must be the sudden rain after so many weeks of sunshine.

People often say to me: 'what on earth do you do all day and night, alone in that cottage?' To me, that's an odd question. For example, I came up to the bedroom for a book, calling into the bathroom on my way. A large spider was fighting a self defeating battle in the wash basin. Like all of us, he was struggling and getting nowhere. So, I put down my book, found a glass and piece of paper, opened the window, and carefully helped him into the glass and out of the window. Then I noticed another one lying on top of the water in the toilet! Thinking he must be dead, I lifted him onto a toilet tissue. He immediately started running, so I dropped him and tissue into basin. Then, using tumbler and paper, I sent him to join his friend. This took an hour, and all I'd done was fetch a book! I spent the next hour marvelling on spiders. How did he stay alive in water like that? Life is full of miracles...

May is almost gone. I drove home from Lancaster in an incredible thunder-storm. Hard spears of rain aimed themselves at my car, glinting in the headlights. The sky, black, night-filled, became illuminated, flooded with flashes of light. Down the lane I drove at two miles per hour behind a wet and frightened stoat, hump-backed in panic as he searched for a gap in the hedgerow.

June

The first day of June, and the wood is densely green and wet. Rain seems never to stop, but as the day is warm, the wood steams like a jungle. Suddenly, it is still - silent. The rain and gales have abruptly gone as rudely as they arrived, leaving behind them a trail of devastation. Lupins, foxgloves, peonies, all lying in defeat on the sodden earth. This evening it is a peaches and cream sky, melting into apricot and then into gold. Clouds become grey mountains - pools left behind by an ebbing sea are golden mirrors reflecting infinity. Now, it is dusk; the lane half shrouded in night. Silent - all around me, still, and silent. Somewhere a cow lows, seagulls quarrel, but around me - silence. Bats, night phantoms, dart, appearing from nowhere, disappearing into the night. The sky streaked amber, grey, darker grey - the moon, full and round is wrapping mysterious halos around the trees. Owl calls echo into the silence.

June has arrived bringing showery weather - and there is still a chill in the air. I have had to batten down my tall plants against the spiteful winds coming from the sea. A wagtail pays me daily visits, his tail wagging up and down to the music of blackbirds and thrushes. A pair of wrens have made their nest on the wood's edge, and spend all day sending out warning calls. A welcome sight this morning was the woodpecker, but he left quickly when he saw there were no nuts left on the bird table.

After many days of dull wetness, the sun this morning rested contentedly on new mown fields, stretched lazily, and smiled. The fields have been combed, their green tresses now lying in neat furrows of gold. In the wood, the sun became cool, dappled, leaving pools of light in dark places.

Ten in the evening, and the day is loath to go. Grey haze clings to the fields, the sky, flushing peach slowly fading into grey. Walking along the lane to Warton Crag, the pace is leisurely - both me and the dog still feeling the easy atmosphere of the day. Air smells fresh, rain-washed.

Country chaos this afternoon! Sheep were being moved from one field to another. They pushed, jostled and complained loudly as they filled the lane, their feet sounding like a sudden shower of rain. It was close and heavy, sun lurking behind leaden storm clouds. It felt difficult to breathe in the still air.

Whoever said that the country-side was quiet and peaceful? Sitting outside I analysed the sound. A cockerel crowed - answered at intervals by another. The sheep complained, birds sang to each other, the tractor droned lazily. An orchestral country symphony, and I love every note.

Tea time, and the leaden clouds, becoming too heavy, release rain in straight steady torrents to the accompaniment of rumbling thunder, the rumbles becoming a prelude to jagged flashes of light flashing across the sky. Cats who had been sleeping in cool corners, raced for shelter, ears back in alarm.

Hedgerows have changed from their Spring colours of blue and yellow into the pink and white of early Summer. Dog-rose and campion, stitchwort and moon daisy have taken the place of celandine, primrose and violet.

Life in a country cottage is full of unexpected surprises. Next doors' cats are constant visitors, just as at home here as there. They each have two names. My name for the little patchy kitten is Motley, and she has just produced kittens. Poor Motley, she is still a baby herself. I was upset to be told that two of the litter had disappeared, but after helping to look, we presumed that Motley had decided to move them. Going back into the kitchen, I was greeted by such a mess. Plants everywhere! Then - a faint sound. Was it one of my cats inadvertently shut in somewhere? I followed the frantic mewing, to discover two kittens neatly stowed away in the back of my large old-fashioned radio. Because my neighbour was out, I was left to baby-sit for the next few hours. A dropper, some diluted evaporated milk, and a willing warm Labrador to nestle up to, and we managed quite well. Motley must have decided to move her family in, but got disturbed mid-move.

June 21st - the longest day. I have sat for an hour watching the sky change from leaden grey into silver, and now, at 10.30pm, it is still quite light - the sky grey merging into brilliant glowing amber. Despite the raucous cries of gulls feeding at the Bird Reserve a mile away, the air is still and silent. Still warm - it brushed against me on my walk with Beau along the waiting lane. Owls calling, were waiting for night to finally spread her dark fingers across the flaming sky, just as I was.

After a wet night, the frog in the kitchen was no great surprise this morning. The cats were gathered round it looking puzzled and wary. A tentative tap from a curious paw sent the frog scurrying under the cooker. Now worms, I am used to - Maui brings her delivery of worms on a daily basis. May Bugs are a May speciality - but frogs is taking things too far. I banished the cats, and played a waiting game for Jeremy Fisher. He emerged after a few minutes, so I swooped him up before he had a chance to hide again. He looked much happier in my small pond. The morning excitement over, five cats returned to their washing and sleeping.

The rain stayed all day, so when the evening became still and clear, I walked through lane and wood. For no reason, I ran - making the trees shiver, spilling their last raindrops onto my face. It smelt so good - reminiscent of rain-water in the water butt of my childhood. Cocooned in green, I watched swifts, or were they swallows, performing aerial acrobatics across the lane.

Lanes are now in full flower. Foxgloves reaching skywards, Hedgerows heavy with elderberry, milky-green tinged. Fields have been mowed, long grass lying in neat green furrows waiting to be gathered. For most of the morning, five cats have sat in a solemn silent circle - staring at a corner of the garden. Though I have looked closely, I can see nothing to hold their attention for so long. Their patience and persistence always amaze me.

JUNE

The early morning wood has a breathless feel, as if I need to tread carefully so as not to disturb a fairy-land. Tentative fingers of sunlight curl around waiting trees, touching the leaves gently - then becoming bolder, make golden pools on the woodland floor. Leaves shudder with pleasure, sun reflecting rainbows in morning dew. The evening wood is still and warm in the failing light of a sunny day. Arums rise up from a sea of blue and green, their pale green hoods translucent in the half light. A perfect end to a perfect day. I walk back to the cottage with a feeling of nostalgia, things almost remembered, memories almost recalled. Elusive feelings slipping in and out of my mind.

Soot everywhere this morning! Cobweb had decided to investigate the chimney. He had climbed up from the fire grate and just a tail tip was showing. I had no time to waste, so I pulled! A very dirty and indignant cat spent the next few hours washing and grooming.

This morning's bird song was joyous, very early, and very loud! I arose to its music at 4.30am, to view an otherwise unseen world. The air was full of activity, and what appeared to be birds, on closer scrutiny turned out to be pipistrelle bats wheeling and flying their intricate swift zigzag patterns. Soon, they would sleep, probably in the disused chimney at Moss House Farm - which was once a Pumping Station used to drain the opposite fields. Then, the day shift takes to the sky - robins, finches, wrens, tits, blackbirds, thrushes, heron, gulls. To watch dawn rise over the cliffs of Jack Scout, to hear the world awakening, is such a privilege

Wrens have spent a busy week building a nest of leaves in my front door gable. One wren working hard to bring the raw material while his lady sifted it through - and rejected most of it. The nest was then meticulously lined with moss - and then abandoned! The wrens must have found a more up-market site.

Such a to-do this morning. I awoke to a garden full of sheep and lambs happily treading on my daffodils and leaving their woolly coats on the bushes. Poor Beau, she was afraid of them, and ran into the kitchen, tail between her legs - what a disaster for a big Labrador. My cats are afraid of birds, and my dog is afraid of sheep.

This time of the year my garden is a constant source of magic and discovery. Underneath bushes and fallen leaves, violets, oxslip and cowslip peep out. Each day brings a new pleasure. While doing some deep digging, I unearthed small toads still hibernating. They sat in my hand, warm and dry, eyeing me steadily. I found a nice hole and popped them into it. Digging has to be left now until the danger of hurting or disturbing them has passed.

On an early morning walk today, I was deafened by the frantic sound of birds feeding on the shore-line. An aerial battle was taking place as the heron unwisely encroached on gull territory, and was forced noisily away. It flew off, lonely and dejected, to find other places. On my return journey I surprised another heron in the narrow water inlets. He rose before me through the morning mist, merging into the greyness.

Flaming June - as cold as a day in Winter! Each small flower closed tightly, waiting for an elusive sun. Walking along a twisted path, I looked across at Leighton Moss. The trees here are Tolkein-like, their twisted trunks standing guard over Leighton Hall, which rests securely in the hollow as it has done for centuries. The first dwelling here was built in the 12th century, the cellars of the Hall going back to that time. I rested for a while by a huge boulder that had an ever-lasting quality, and I wondered how long it had been there. In the field beyond, a tree had embedded itself in a rock. The rock having split in two with the tree still flourishing, though on its side - such tenacity!

Deepdale wood proved a greater temptation today than the garden. The wood is a wonderful secret place. Rocky crags to which both trees and ferns cling with verdant determination. Out from the green arms of the wood, to marvel at the graceful sweep of fields ahead. Beau was carefully balancing a large stick, which was fine until she tried to get it through the gates! Back into the wood again - the path over-grown, a riotous tangle of flowers and thorns spilling over each other. Foxgloves are in bud, and will soon be the royalty of the wood. One more stop to admire the view (and to re-gain lost breath) looking down to Storr's Moss glistening in the distance. Back now to Leighton Hall, up the hill, with very frequent pauses to revel in the sweeping fields, and the Hall itself sitting in dignified grandeur at the bottom. The view from here is so varied - Storr's Moss, the drained area of Leighton Moss marsh, then still on to Morecambe Bay and the hills of the Lake District.

An insect tonight, clinging to my mirror, pale emerald, delicate, eyes made of gold, wings - a whisper of silver lace, defied the laws of gravity, fragile legs gripping as he admired his beauty.

Late June - 'Blue and green should never be seen' - the old adage came back into my mind as I looked up at a blue sky through a green lace curtain of leaves, then down to a spreading carpet of bluebells - shaded again by the darker green canopy of branches. This was a time of reflection - a time when echoes from the past were louder, nearer than this moment. More tangible than a tomorrow as yet unknown.

June is ending dismally. The odd sunny day is linked by days of wind and rain, lanes littered with branches - my garden, flattened.

A trip to the Lyth Valley was rewarded by the sight of butterfly orchids, waxy cream petals tilted upwards. Pyramid orchids clustered around them. On our return home, a small deer ran across the lane, bringing a cry of delight from my daughter, who was visiting from the city. I'm not sure I feel quite so delighted when I go to look for my lilies and see all the new shoots nibbled by my evening visitors. Still, it's a big garden, and the honour of sharing it with deer, rabbits, moles and many more creatures far out-weighs the lost buds.

A bird was tapping in a demanding fashion at the window this morning. No doubt feeling too lazy to find his own food, and wondering where the Winter supply of nuts and bird seed cakes had gone. Moles have begun to inhabit the vegetable plot. Never mind - there is room for us all I guess. Toads are now appearing nightly by the back door, so it's essential to tread very carefully. At least they like the wet weather.

July

My secret wood looked sad. Enchanter's night-shade and dog's mercury drooped wearily onto each other. Trees gave up their leaves, allowing them to drift hopelessly to the ground. So long since there was any rain, and this lonely secret place was slowly dying. Ferns no longer curled, but hung down in melancholy despair. Easy now to hear tiny shrews scurrying, as dry brown leaves - old before their time, rustled to every touch. The wood was patient, waiting.

Today, the rain fell. It began tentatively, gaining confidence until it became a steady grey downpour. It clung to branches in moist crystal droplets, bounced joyfully onto dry leaves, rested on the dusty ground - filling the searing gaping wounds lying open in jagged cracks. It caressed the drooping greenery, coaxing it into new life. Now the wood was crying - awash with tears. These were tears of relief, as my beloved wood shuddered, sighed, and came to life again.

The 4th of July, Independence Day, and the American flag flies on Warton Church in honour of the illustrious Washington family, whose forebears now rest in the Warton Churchyard. It flutters limply in the constant rain. Fields are looking very green. Raindrops drip crystals as I brush the branches in passing.

JULY

A humid but damp day, and a walk in Kentmere had to be abandoned because of flies - never have I seen so many! They clustered around my head, getting into ears, eyes and nose - buzzing angrily. It was like an Alfred Hitchcock film. Clouds of grey silk draped over the hills - fields became emeralds, spikes of ruby willow herb and foxglove reaching upwards. Grey misty-laced cobwebs on hedges, diamonds clinging to emerald grasses.

Today the sun was warm, but wind blew across from Jack Scout cliffs turning long grass into a waving green sea. By Woodwell, ragged robin grew; Meadow Brown butterflies rested on meadow sweet. The musky smell became intoxicating as I walked across this magic meadow. Slender grasses parting to reveal another world of insects. Eye to eye with a tiny green grass-hopper, I knelt down and peered into his world. He paused a-while in his singing to peer back at me through his dense green grass jungle, before springing deftly away and disappearing.

Yesterday, I walked in sun, now I look out onto a windswept landscape. Gale force winds are blowing across the Bay to flatten my struggling flowers. Sudden downpours of rushing rain playing hide and seek with the sun. Disregarding the rain, a mother pheasant paraded proudly along the lane with her three chicks. Now, this evening, walking in my wood with the dog, it is deep, dank, and full of mystery. Green blending into darker green; green underfoot, green above and around me. Rain dripping down my neck from branches. An up-rooted tree lying with leaves still fresh. I found an undiscovered part of the wood beyond the old mine shaft. Very craggy and steep, slippery limestone rocks disguised in green moss. Honeysuckle trailing from overhead branches.

Suddenly it is hot! Sunshine causing the wetness to rise in steamy mists. Flowers that had remained tight-closed, now burst into glorious blossom, the garden becoming a colourful paradise. Greylag geese are back again in the newly mown field which I have watched in its every stage. With the sun, comes the flies and midges.

We seem to be caught in a heat-wave. As there is also a light breeze, it is perfect. I stood to watch a small white butterfly lay her eggs on the nasturtiums. A Tortoiseshell butterfly has gone to sleep on a picture frame on the stairs. Fields shimmer under the heat haze. Mornings begin softly, a cobweb mist lying across the fields. Toads burrow for coolness, and the cats laze their day away under the buddleia bush, occasionally dabbing half-heartedly at butterflies.

The deer have been into my garden during the night, nibbling young shoots from trees and shrubs, and eating my eagerly awaited lily buds. Moles have now reached the vegetable patch. I live in a guarded truce with field mice, rabbits, moles, deer, birds, slugs and snails. Each night at midnight, I go into the garden with a bucket, gather up all visible slugs and snails, then carry them into the heart of the wood. My theory is, that they take so long to travel, it'll give the garden a fighting chance.

It is in the 90's! Small Tortoiseshell, Red Admiral, Meadow Brown and small White butterflies fill the air. They flit delicately from buddleia to nasturtium, conducting aerial ballets as they dip and soar. Bees, heads down, buzz solemnly about the serious business of gathering pollen, bottoms up in each flower. A cat moves indignantly as she is disturbed from her sleep on the outhouse roof by thrushes bombarding her with cherry stones from next door's tree. Cleo, having moved slowly away to have an unconcerned wash, the thrushes now bombard me. How magical it is to watch the sun set over Heald Brow at 9pm. Everything rests - even the greylags have become silent.

When my friend Lesley Rose rang to say he had discovered thousands of orchids, I thought he was exaggerating - but he wasn't. I walked across the disused quarry and sand heaps into a fairy-land. How breathtaking! Not thousands, but millions of perfect orchids. There were at least four varieties - Common spotted, Northern Fen, Early Marsh and Marsh among them. They wore colours from white through to deepest purple. The quarry had become a living carpet, as orchids wove into Birdsfoot Trefoil, Self-Heal, Bush Vetch, Lesser Trefoil, Hop Trefoil, Crosswort, Hedge Woundwort, Goosegrass, Red Clover - and so many more.

This morning I was faced with a vegetarian's dilemma - such chaos in my kitchen. I opened the kitchen drawer, looked in amazement at two small bright eyes, and promptly closed the drawer, disbelief on my face. I opened it a second time to look at the tiny mouse face. We studied each other for a very long minute before the mouse, gaining his instincts for survival. disappeared into the bowels of my cupboard. There now followed an hour of frantic activity as the kitchen was systematically dismantled. Each time one cupboard was removed, the mouse scurried behind another. The dog got very excited, and had to be evicted into the garden, as I kept falling over her. Sheldon, my black cat, strolled in amidst the chaos, ate his breakfast - and strolled out again! The mouse was terrified - it sat huddled in an in-accessible corner behind the cooker. The kitchen was re-assembled, and a decision made to leave the safari until the following day, having removed all food from reach and throwing out what Mr. Mouse had left me of the biscuits. The following morning I approached the dilemma in a more scientific way. As I pulled out each cupboard, I sealed the escape route with masking tape. The dog was again outside, her nose poking through the cat-flap, just to watch events. Sheldon was lounging on the couch together with Sultan and Simkins. Having left only one escape route, I positioned myself at the end - large basin at the ready. The unwelcome lodger was gently urged towards it. In a last little panic, he shot forward into the basin, and I slid a plate over the top. Triumphantly I carried the mouse into the wood, removed the plate, and watched him run to freedom. Looking bemused, the little bundle of brown fur emerged, paused to look at his liberator. Bright eyes watching me, he scurried gratefully into the wood. In the cottage, three cats slept soundly, totally oblivious to the drama just enacted. I now intend to eliminate unreachable corners in readiness for the next field mouse looking for free lodgings.

The past few days of July have been full of sun, bees and flowers. Living by the sea, fragrant air was lifted on a breeze, dispersing the heady scent of honeysuckle, orange-blossom and rose. Already, I am having to water the special plants. Cobweb, my grey kitten, has had great fun chasing flies on the window, while the three older cats choose to lie in shady spots in the garden - their idleness shared by the three cats from next door. The moon tonight was full and clear, lighting up the lane, exposing owls and bats on their nocturnal flights.

All traffic came to an abrupt halt this morning - to allow a duck, a drake and six ducklings to stroll up the lane at a leisurely pace, looking for a gap in the hedge leading to the sea. No rush or panic, the drake supervised his family to safety with dignity. It is in moments such as this that I feel great warmth to my fellow men. Not everyone in the world is without care. Everyone waited patiently, no-one pipped a horn, and the incident brought indulgent smiles as cars slowly moved off again.

Was it only yesterday that I walked in sunshine? Tea time, and my door is firmly shut against the driving rain. Cats, dog and me - fire crackling, watch as rain is hurled at the windows by a howling wind. Such fury in contrast to the gentleness of yesterday. Sky and field merge into a misty grey, no end and no beginning. The soft pink rose that had opened its petals, now drooped - pink petals tossed thoughtlessly onto the wet earth.

Sun and rain had chased each other all day, making it feel more like

April than July. The tide at Arnside came in at various angles as always, but today it raced in, tripped and rolled onto the shore, the more usual insidious creeping abandoned. A cold wind urged it on, and chased grey clouds across the sky. Newly cut verges smelled of garlic and aniseed, where ramsons and sweet cicely had been growing. I found my usual pleasure in finding pineapple mayweed underfoot. Such an enticing smell when pressed between fingers. So many things to see, to watch, to find, to smell, to listen to. The capricious weather adding the pleasure of the unexpected to my walk. Wet grass soaked my feet and legs, but I went on, unaware of discomfort. A young pheasant, the colour of wet sand, ran out in front of me.

Midnight in the lane, soft darkness seeming like a solid black wall, melted before me, wrapped around me. This was a different world, and I was the intruder. Greylags in the far field still argued, endlessly and noisily. Gulls feeding at the sea's edge made a continuous sound - no longer querulous, just sleepy. I bent to rescue a toad, his mouth full of slug - putting him on the grassy verge to finish his supper. This is my special time, shared with my old Labrador. It's all she can manage now. Her days of racing along the shore, just a memory. What is the magic? Is it that feeling of adventure - an excursion into a night world of prowling cats, melancholy hooting of owls, scurrying of rabbits and voles? It is warm still. Now - moths of many shapes and sizes fly in frenzied circles. Bats swoop in graceful curves. They pass me by so swiftly, it becomes unreal. Did I imagine the shadow? I stood still, feeling secure in night's gentleness - letting the hurrying flights move around me, resting in the cacophony of bird calls, sheep bleats. Stepping carefully over slugs and snails, the dog and me headed for the garden gate. Time to leave the night to its mysteries.

Another normal morning! A mouse carefully placed on the kitchen mat by cat number four. A chewed houseplant and ripped wall-paper - the culprit, a small grey dynamo kitten misnamed Cobweb! Yesterday was a warm and wet day. Rain steadily fell all day, a continuous curtain. This morning, the still wet wood shines luminous green. An intense depth of green, glowing - inviting. Enormous slugs and brazen snails lie on garden paths and decorate the outhouse door. The purple buddleia, flourishes from the roof of the outhouse, thriving on nothing, while the one in garden soil, nurtured and loved - languishes. The two little girls from the bottom cottage have arrived to play on my swing that hangs in a wood clearing from a strong old tree. They always ask first, which is special.

Today, they have four friends, so, feeling that really is four too many, I went to sort it out. It seemed that their arrow had lodged in the tree, so we spent an enjoyable ten minutes throwing stones up to dislodge it. Mission accomplished, they went on their way. Tea time, and two small girls call again, this time to show me the seascape they had made from sawdust, mint leaves, stones and pipe-cleaners on an old board.

Where did Summer go? For days it has rained. Now, the wind is cold, the sky looks heavy and angry - with only the flowers to remind me it is Summer. They bend in the wind, all that they can do. Rose petals swirl and fall, pink convolvulus cling to the hedge, their tenacity belying their delicacy. Leaves, torn prematurely from the trees, joined the rose petals in their dancing. Branches tossed defiantly, showering me with unwanted raindrops.

Travelling home very late along the dark, wet lane, my headlights illuminating rain, spearing the windscreen with perfectly symmetrical arrows - looking like iron filings drawn to a magnet. I screeched to a sudden stop. Lying in the road, spot-lighted by my headlights, were two tiny kittens. They were huddled together in a pathetic bundle of wet fur. I went to pick them up, their mewing, plaintive and loud. Thin and bedraggled, they had probably been abandoned. I scooped them up, taking them to the cottage. My sleek well fed cats were horrified. Cobweb stared indignantly at the newcomers, Sheldon stalked around them, Sultan sat aloof, indifferent - hiding his curiosity behind a raised paw. Cleo spat as always. My oldest cat, she has no time for the young. I fed the kittens, cuddled them, and made them a cosy bed in the out-house. Time enough in the morning to take the next step of passing them on to Gabby Oldfield of RSPCA rescue, for re-homing.

Late noon and the sun has at last made the reluctant clouds smile. My walk past Jenny Brown's Point was a warm but still gusty one. As always, my walk seemed to reach Wolf House Gallery, where I had the best cup of coffee and scone in Lancashire, and a warm friendly chat with Ted and Denise, before heading back over Heald Brow. The wind was still blowing. How amazing that the most delicate flowers choose the harshest places and seasons in which to display themselves. Snowdrops defy the frost and snow, violets hide away in hedges, and dainty harebells cling to windy hills and crags - holding on despite harsh winds and playful breezes.

It was one of those grey days so typical of English Summers. The grey-stoned buildings of ancient Lancaster looked even more grey with their back-drop of leaden clouds. I walked through the town hungry for colour, and found even more than I needed to sate my dulled appetite. An Asian wedding was in progress. Suddenly, the sullen streets were vibrant with colour, pulsating with life and sound. The entire Asian community had gathered busily to celebrate a wedding. Was it a special one I wondered, or a good reason to get in touch with culture, and to bring some Asian sunshine into our grey country? Such colours, as women gathered in noisy groups – saris of red, aglow with golden thread, the blue of night skies sparkling with a thousand silver stars, soft white, austere black - mingled in a burst of colour. Children in their very best, black hair in shining braids, excitement spilling from them. The sound of singing, talking, quelled traffic noise into an insignificant grumble, as Lancaster paused, watched, and made a space for its Asian community to paint colour onto a grey morning.

A wonderful hot day followed by a warm wet day, has created a steamy damp world in the garden. Freshly made cement has proved a new and fascinating wonder for the cats. After lots of cautious investigation, Cobweb lifted the polythene (placed to protect it) neatly with one fat paw, allowing Daisy and Lux to have a really good look. I now have autographed concrete.

This evening, a walk round my garden before bedtime, revealed another world. Soft warm rain rested on the pink roses, glistened in the light from the cottage windows. The toads are back. Last year there were fewer than usual, but amongst the wet leaves, the herb garden tonight was alive with tiny perfect baby toads. I stooped to watch them, so busy in their nocturnal activities. Snails and slugs were everywhere - huge snails, bigger than the toads.

The hot weather continues. It's so good to wake up each day to the brightness and the blue sky. The 'Cobweb Garden' (my new secure cat garden) has become a haven for the cats. They lie blissfully around, punctuating their days with sporadic bursts of hide and chase. In the early evening, they spend long moments watching night moths and insects. The cat frame made from rustic poles, complete with sitting platforms, is a great success. They run to the top, dive on each other, scratch claws, then sit at different levels to watch the day go by, and to wash.

Butterflies are in short supply this year. I can only think it must be to do with the weather conditions - but then - I am British.

After a perfect, hot day with a shimmering heat haze hovering over the sea, it was good to sit with the cats in Cobweb's garden with my supper. The air, still warm, moved slowly around me, resting on my skin like a silken shawl. Moths flew close to the grass, making tempting targets for cats. Their amazing aerobatics meant that they were never caught. Sitting silent in the still garden, an owl hooted just above me. Looking up to the over-hanging trees, I saw him. Neither of us moved for a long moment, then, he spread magnificent wings, rose slowly, and flew off into the night. Happiness is experiencing moments such as this.

August

August already; in waterproof jacket and ear-muffs I set out for Heald Brow. Lapwings soared and dived over the field, melancholy cries belying ecstatic aerobatics. Wind sent grey clouds scudding across the sky. The sun peeped out, deciding whether to smile or hide. Deciding to smile, she pushed back the heavy clouds, and beamed

July was a wonderful hot month, evidently the hottest since 1600 and something. Now, July has gone, leaving a trail of temperamental thunder storms in her wake. The day began hot and sultry, but by early afternoon, began to sulk, pout and grumble. Cats sleeping in abandoned positions under shrubs, became suddenly alert as thunder rumbled, gained power, and finally burst above us. They didn't wait for the jagged lightning arrows which tore the sky apart - but ran into the safety of the cottage. Shrubs raised their leaves and smiled. Starved of water, the storm was welcome. A final roar and its attendant flash of lightening, robbed Crag Foot of its electricity! Hours later, the silence of the early evening cottage was stirred, as radio and lights burst once more into life.

The rain this morning was very welcome. It's still warm and sultry -

the atmosphere has become steamy and feels tropical. By lunchtime, the sun was shining in all its glory. Flowers opened and butterflies became very busy - Peacock, Meadow Brown, Tortoiseshell and White butterflies chased each other from flower to flower.

Ninety degrees and still soaring! The heat is a moving wall, it settles around my body like a clinging blanket. Grass turns to straw, and the cats move restlessly to find shelter. Simkins brought me a live mole this morning, the same size as himself, and he didn't know how to deal with it. Softly grey, little hands set backwards for digging, pink snout twitching. He was very frightened, yet bravely struggled in my hand until he reached my fingers, where he landed a nasty bite. I released him into the wood and he promptly tunnelled downwards.

Walking along the lane during the afternoon, I enjoyed the shade of trees. A deer wandered across in front of me, too hot to rush. This hot sultry weather is bringing a variety of insects and moths into the cottage. Tiny jewels in green and silver. A moth, mustard gold with peach stripes on his wings, peach legs and large eyes, has settled onto the mirror. The cleg fly is also on form, as my swollen leg and foot show. Thank goodness, today there is a breeze. Everywhere is so dry. The usual rock pools and crevices on Jack Scout are dusty, which puzzles the dog, who enjoys her splashes in them. A family of swans, four cygnets swam neatly down the centre of a very narrow stream. A sheep trotted purposefully up to me as I crossed the field towards the woods. He allowed me to give his head a scratch. Arriving at Wolf House Gallery, a lovely place to sit with a drink and home-made cake, I was amused to watch the peacock strutting amongst visitors enjoying the admiration.

Such unpredictable weather; it's possible in one day to experience Spring, Summer, Autumn and even Winter. After days of lazy heat, now, it's wet and very windy - the sea frothed into galloping white horses. Poor garden! Bending to the wind, when yesterday it stretched in sunshine. There are two tortoiseshell butterflies on my study ceiling, closed and waiting.

Rain has visited daily, making grass and trees lush and green, the sea - spirited. The cliffs of Jack Scout are a moist green carpet, bursting with colourful life. Tiny eyebright, meadow cranesbill, thyme and rockrose. Mullein, having found a secret crevice in the limestone rocks, rose upwards - tall golden spikes giving away its hiding place. Trailing St. John's wort, tormentil, harebells, yarrow, dropwort, storksbill, self-heal - so many flowers thriving here. I stood to look across the wind-lashed sea. The tide receded, leaving rocks bare - sand, still.

I have found a part of the Lakes as yet quiet and unspoiled. The narrow lane I walked along was edged high with creamy Meadowsweet and rosebay willowherb. Ox-eye daisies tangled and fell onto the lane, brushing my legs with raindrops. Sun touched the hedges, reaching through moist green trees stretching to reach each other over-head. It dried their leaves, and made for me, a dappled shade. Wild raspberries made a tasty treat, one to share with the birds, who had beaten me to it, but still left a few. I leaned over a gate to be licked by a huge soft-eyed cow. Braver than the others, her curiosity got the better of her. She licked my hand, scratched her back on the post, then, losing interest, she wandered away to join her friends.

Getting out for a walk is becoming a battle of wits between me and the cats. They follow me down the garden path, knowing I will go back, give them a saucer of milk, then retreat quickly before they follow again! Today, it is distinctly Autumnal. Recent rain has perked up the wilting wood, and the air is beginning to have a scent of wood fires.

Standing in the wood tonight, wrapped in darkness, it became another world. The wood was alive with sounds. Two foxes holding a noisy conversation, frightened the dog, making her hackles rise as she joined in the barking. Owls called as they searched the night for supper. Shrews scurried underfoot, toads rustled in the undergrowth. My cats, no longer domestic and wide-eyed, now slid silently past me, disappearing into the enveloping darkness.

Suddenly, it is hot again. The air humid and tropical, with a haze hovering over Jack Scout cliffs. Wasps are getting aggressive and drowsy. Mornings and evenings playing a prelude to Autumn. Bryony has twined necklaces of yellow hearts around tree trunks. The first leaves have turned from green to gold. Soon, the bryony hearts will fall to the ground, leaving shiny red bead necklaces decorating bare tree trunks.

Lambs were still suckling and staying close to Mum, even though they were by now the same size! A group of stoical cows huddled around the stile, so I pushed my way through. Their disinterested stare followed me across, and they quickly returned to their leisurely munching. I sat on the hill-side of Heald Brow to look across wet fields, seeing my cottage sitting securely on the edge of Windy Scout Brow Wood.

Already halfway through August, and still it rains. Leaves are looking prematurely Autumnal. Spring this year seems to have welcomed

AUGUST

Autumn and ignored Summer completely.

The constant rain has been paradise for slugs and snails. They lie outside the back door - down the garden path, every colour from pale beige to black, and in all sizes. They make walking outside very hazardous in the dark. This evening I set about my usual job of collecting them into a bucket for transportation to the wood. I have found lots of tiny toads, no bigger than my thumb nail, and black, hopping in and out of the slugs, (they could be frogs). I shall leave some slugs in case the toads are hungry. Three enormous snails on a voyage up the shed door can wait until tomorrow.

Another small soft grey mole lay on the grass this morning, no marks on him at all. I have been blaming the cats, but this is the third unmarked mole to appear - so maybe they have been poisoned.

After days of endless rain, this morning, the world was new. It was held in a timeless moment in a spot-light of sun reaching through the woodland trees. Shining ferns and leaves - causing them to shudder with delight, and sending a shimmering ripple through cobwebs which laced among branches. All the rain of recent weeks had given the grass an extra spurt of growth, making it thick and lush. Mowing it made more problems, as buried in it were tiny toads. I decided to abandon grass cutting in favour of toads

The butterflies today were many, and I spent long moments watching them go in fickle flight from one flower to another. Somewhere on the edge of the wood, a wren was singing - a song of such sweetness and intensity. In the porch, a tortoiseshell butterfly has attached itself to the wall.

The night was full of strange noises. No moon, stars cloaked in cloud, the lane was a solid immovable wall. I stood - still; was that an owl? It didn't sound like an owl. Scurrying close to my feet - squeaks. A strange mixture of silence and sound. By the hedge, a sound of shuffling, grunting - getting nearer. Dogs, usually silent, barked incessantly. A disembodied voice from somewhere yelled at the dogs, but still they barked. How could a night be so empty and yet so alive? I thought I knew every mood of this place, yet tonight, all is new and strange again. I thought back to childhood stories of giant leeches slushing from an unseen swamp, told to me with great relish by my big brother.

I marvelled at the sea this morning as it lay heavy, alight with the shine of a myriad diamonds, and, for a moment, I glimpsed eternity.

A RIOT OF THORN AND LEAF

A day of sparkling splendour. I walked by Leighton Hall, looking across to the Lakeland Hills, outlined against the sky in crystal clarity. A wonderful painting in blue, green and white - such a welcome contrast to grey. Dew rested on leaves, sun rested on water. Hedges were already heavy with blackberries, cobnuts. This is a time of richness - seas of silk and velvet in gold and amber. The smell of ripe hay mingled with honeysuckle and nostalgic breaths of wood-smoke.

The end of another hot day, and I sat looking across the Bay. The sky had turned from clear blue to aquamarine, flushing deepest orange, fading to palest peach. Mirrored in a still sea, the water flooded orange. A single boat lay on its side, its dark shape stark against the flaming sea. It looked lonely, yet peaceful. As the sky darkened with night - the full glowing moon became surrounded by golden rings of light.

Little grey cat - I watched you as you picked your way through morning grass, cobweb laced and crystal spangled. Each paw lifted high, shaken, and placed down with grace. Tentative, pausing to test the air, fresh and new to your wondering. Your first journey into a shining sun spangled world, and a cat garden created especially for you. A butterfly tantalisingly settled on a flower, soaring upwards as you reached to investigate with a hesitant paw. Getting braver now, a sudden run into this magical new world through rustling grasses. This is 'Cobweb's Garden'.

My morning walk felt more like Autumn, despite it still being August. A mist rested on Warton Crag, disguising the trailing cobwebs which brushed my face. There was a smell of musk, heavy and oriental. A few blackberries, early-ripe, graced hedgerows. Bryony leaves were turning yellow, and it all seemed in too much haste for me.

A tortoiseshell butterfly has taken up residence in a corner of my bedroom ceiling. In a troubled world, the simple pleasure of such an honour is extreme.

Night-time in the Summer lane - too early for bats and owls, but shiny brown slugs lie boldly on the road. A few moths have begun to move the evening air, brushing against my face. The pale pink convolvulus that grace the hedges, have tight-closed, their smiling trumpets now furled into slender shapes. An evening lane can seem a lonely place. Solitary bird calls echo from the marsh, muzzy twitterings in hedges as small birds settle for the night, and rustling in the grass as nocturnal mammals wake up. This is the night shift, preparing for their world. I walked across the Crag through a shaded tunnel of trees. Beyond, where the trees ended, open grass-land glowed golden in the fading light.

Slugs have been another problem this Summer. Huge slugs in many colours have sat on the back porch, mountaineered the front steps, and leered from outhouse doors. They have proved to be too much for the toads to deal with, but have been a diversion for cats. Cobweb has spent hours watching the slow advance of a slug on the garden path. Daisy May brings them in, and four cats sit in consultation around them, dabbing occasionally with a paw, until I remove them.

Last day of August, and cake baking has become a hazardous business. Wasps invade my kitchen, zooming around me making angry noises. A bee-keeper's hat would be more useful than an apron!

September

utumn has arrived quietly, trailing her pale gold skirts across the hedgerows, draping grey cobweb lace between its leaves. She has hung crystals onto the cobweb lace, then gracefully draped her red bryony beads around them. Her musky damp perfume floated behind her. She was still - waiting.

Summer has, just as quietly left, leaving Autumn to take her place. Days are sunny, but it is the molten gold of Autumn now that turns the still sea to a glimmering expanse. Chestnut trees, always the first, have dressed themselves in shades of yellow and rust. Bryony berries begin to blush, and there is the smell of wood-smoke mingling with fallen leaves in the air.

Cobweb is spared the indignity of forcing himself through the now too small cat-flap, as the door is open wide. Yesterday he caused a queue as he heaved his bulk through - and got wedged! The other three cats had to wait while I assisted.

The steady rhythmic beat of wings made me look up in time to see a pair of swans flying overhead. Walking slowly along the lane, I buried myself in this golden world, too mellow and gentle to hurry in, too dignified and beautiful not to feel in awe of. If Autumn is the old age of the year, then how can old age be an ugly thing?

Home again, I watched rain-drops on my window pane. They hung, crystalline tear-drops, pausing for a small space in time before falling down and transforming into a million sparkling rainbows.

The rain is falling again today, soft and steady. Clouds draped grey silk across the hills, the intense green of fields and trees made sharp contrast for the tall spikes of willow herb reaching skyward. Cobwebs meticulously spun between hedgerow twigs, hung heavy with shining drops of rain. The cats are at their most perverse - asking for exit at the back door, seeing rain, then running to the front door, convinced it will be fine. They glare steady-eyed at me - it's all my fault!

Surprise! It rained again today. The sun did oblige later on though. I am becoming obsessed with weather. Using a map, I did a varied walk across flat plateaus of limestone pavement, through woodland and across fields. The rustle of leaves - I stood still, my caution rewarded with sight of a deer sprinting in front of me. On again, I passed three disgruntled horses sheltering beneath trees; heads dry - bottoms wet. Scarlet pimpernel flowers stayed tight-closed. As a child I was told that they predict rain by refusing to open, which seems to be true.

How different today! Walking on a narrow path on the cliff-tops of Jack Scout, I watched the sea, white horses riding the water, then bursting joyfully against the rocks. I had difficulty in keeping my footing, as the racing wind blew everything in its way.

The strong winds continued to blow, and the temptation to walk to the cliffs became irresistible. Grey clouds scudded across a leaden sky. Lapwings soared and swooped, silhouetted silver showers across its sullen face.

Mid September - a pale yellow day of intense clarity. Looking back to Crag Foot as I walked to Leighton Moss, the cottage peered out through swirls of grey mist. Cobwebs trailed across my face. At Woodwell, sun lit up the field, showing clearly the colony of cobwebs suspended between reedy grass. They sparkled silver-grey, drooped with the weight of the dew. Ragged robin still grew by the stream. Blackberries hung in lush blue-black clusters, rose-hips glowed red. The day was heavy with the scent of hay, sweet-sour, rich. Mushrooms collected from the field made good soup.

The middle of this month of contrasts - mist shrouded the fields and clung to cobwebs. Warm sun slowly coaxed the mist away, leaving behind a day of shining gold. Bryony berries tangled together with Hip and hawthorn in red splendour. Blackberries in abundance hung grape-like in the hedgerows. The first trees are turning pale yellow and amber - Autumn is tiptoeing in so quietly this year. Tonight, as the sun sets over Jack Scout cliffs, the sky is glowing amber melting into peach and apricot.

Winds have swept across the woods and fields, torn leaves from trees, then left again. Now, the leaves lay where they were tossed - still, in the damp grey morning. Bryony necklaces lace around the hedges. Their pale heart-shaped leaves have joined the others, now clinging wetly to woodland paths.

Autumn is a season of richness, amber, citrine, carnelian, ruby, garnet. The pungent perfume of aniseed where sweet cicely has been cut is rich. The sun shines gently, leaves becoming set in spun gold.

A walk along the lane after tea; orange evening sun had caused trees to blush into deepest orange, remaining pools from an ebbing tide were large golden mirrors. Even the grey-stoned walls warmed to apricot as they too reflected the sun.

Today, the sun was warm, so I set out with my two sons, to walk to Jenny Brown's Point and the Giant's Seat. The very high tide was receding slowly, making it impossible to walk past the chimney. We scrambled up Heald Brow to find our way round. This necessitated climbing over barbed wire fences (no notice to say 'Private'!) Fine for the lads, not so easy for me. With one lifting and one catching, I made it, but not without a few attempts and much laughter. Reaching the Giant's Seat hot and bedraggled, our picnic tasted wonderful. The sea lay still beneath the sun, stretching lazily toward distant hills. A prehistoric looking heron made his solitary flight above us. We decided to carry on to enjoy coffee in Wolf House Gallery. Our return trip was easier as the grass was now just boggy. Lapwings circled over-head, their plaintive calls carrying across the marshes. Reeds stood tall, sending whispered messages to each other. Along the Dyke's edge, sheep ran in front of us complaining loudly about the disturbance. Why is it that I can walk here so often, yet always see something new and different?

Constant rain all day has brought out every slug and snail for miles. Tonight, they climb up my doors, mountaineer the front steps, climb onto the table in the pantry. There was a convention in the Herb Garden - slugs, snails, a few frogs and toads of every size from tiny to huge. I watched this nocturnal gathering for a long time before collecting up the snails and slugs (leaving a few for the toads) and taking them into the wood. Such odd happenings at midnight! I watched a spider eating a large crumb of cat food. This natural world that I share with so many creatures is always amazing.

The world today seems so bloated, as fields lie sodden from rain and high tides, cows stand heavy with milk, blackberries hang heavy in the hedges, streams are swollen.

Walking in the Autumn day, slowly to match the mood of mellowing sun and amber leaves drifting to the ground. The path before me, carpeted amber too. Geese in noisy flight above me, climbing higher and higher in a perfect 'V' formation. Off to their Winter places, flying hundreds of miles - wings beating constantly. This miracle happens each year, and each year I marvel at the instinct that drives them to achieve seemingly impossible feats of strength, endurance and navigation. How could I ever take this world for granted!

Hard lumps beneath my feet reveal tiny yellow crab apples. I fill the large bag from my rucksack, and bring them home. Now, they fill the cottage with the smell of ripe apples, and provide a game for two clumsy cats as they knock the bag over and chase apples across the floor. Tomorrow, the kitchen will smell even better, as I turn my harvest into crab apple jelly.

The crab apples have been transformed into jars of clear amber jelly, and stand in rows on the window sill - the same colour as the Autumn leaves.

Late afternoon sun darted playfully between leaves. Warm Summery wind moved the branches, sharing games with the sun. We cycled along the lane, my young friend and I - me desperately trying to keep up with Tim's fast disappearing figure. Fields became an exciting green blur; I became young again - the wind streaming through my hair, rushing in my ears. Such a feeling of freedom! Brown grassy reeds leaned gracefully over the water, which rippled happily to the wind's song. Green grass bent forward to hear the wind's whispered messages. Lapwings rose and fell above me, captives of the wind. It released them, tossing them aside. Caught in the sudden breath, they swirled suddenly, swiftly away above the newly ploughed fields.

This evening, I walked along the lane which goes over Warton Crag, choosing to walk in the silent dark because it wraps me around, and I feel separate - safe. Following a clear autumnal day, it was still almost warm. Morecambe's lights glittered in the far distance, and I was glad to be up here, just watching them from a long way off. The night-black which looked so solid when I set out, soon became transparent. Now, I could see shadows, as trees took shape. Stars, low in the sky seemed almost to be hanging on still, dark branches. A tiny pinpoint of light moved, fell in a graceful curve, and vanished. Shooting stars that I watched - yet they ceased to exist at least four million years ago. Such mysteries of great magnitude, and here I was, thinking that my own life was so important! All those stars, solar systems, infinite. My life, not even an instant flash of light in a night sky. Walking homewards again, I listened to leaves falling. The hedgerows rustled as mice, shrews, rabbits went about their night-time business. As the darkness melted before me, I thought - maybe in our life's rushes, the darkness that is our confusion and doubt, would also melt if we could just find time to stop, and to listen.

Standing for a moment in a busy day, I watched the river Kent, its waters rushing constantly onwards. It was so completely timeless and unchangeable. It seemed to come from 'forever' and thunder on for ever

- and it has always been so. I could return in a week, a year, or one hundred years, and still that water would be falling ever downwards. Ducks, still caught in its cross-currents, like the debris and fallen leaves of a Summer now gone. But only gone until the Autumn has glowed, and Winter spread her cold white carpet, followed by the green beginning of life once more. So completely and reliably unchangeable. I know quite surely that whatever happens to people, the trees will continue to bud, flower, mellow and rest. The water will still flow and thunder, then lie in silent dark hollows waiting for the secret willows to bow down, reflecting their flowing tresses.

Gentle, apple-gold days, slow and easy, butterflies moving lightly. A Red Admiral honours me by resting on my skirt a-while. Wasps haunt my kitchen, and even jam or honey on a saucer doesn't distract them. The cats stretch out in the sun, languid, lazy. A sudden burst of noise from an overhead aeroplane causes my huge grey cat Cobweb to dash frantically for the safety of the cottage. It looks very funny, as he is the biggest cat and also the biggest coward. In late afternoon sun, I watch a damsel fly hover and rest on the flowers. Now, the ripe peach-blushed sky is fading slowly into the deep blue of evening.

Rain fell all day today - determined and persistent. At midnight it had stopped, but the cloying dampness lingered. Sitting on the front steps, I watched toads of varying sizes hopping between the slugs and snails. Snails were climbing the steps and wall. There seems to be no place they cannot reach. Stumbling about in the wood, I emptied the bucket of collected snails and slugs where they couldn't harm my plants.

What is it about blackberries? I find it impossible to ignore them. Walking along the lane to wrap myself in the warm Autumn sun, and there they were - shining black clusters peeping out from still green bryony berries. Not prepared, I filled my pocket and both hands. A blackberry and apple pie is tonight's treat.

One frantic white cat caused chaos this morning. A lazy wasp had aroused Daisy's curiosity, but her tentative sniff and dab was disaster. The wasp, not wanting her attentions, stung her paw. The result was Daisy - running madly into the cottage knocking over everything in her path. Poor Daisy!

The day was so alive; a breeze, too early to remove leaves not yet wanting to let go of branches, played with them instead. Looking from the lane, the sea lay brightly silver. How could I have set out without my usual plastic bag! Blackberries tempted me from the cover of hedges. No use - I filled my hands until there was no more room. They felt comfortable sitting in the curve of my palm. The hedge-cutter had been before me, and now exposed were pale mauve deadly nightshade flowers. Bryony berries were turning from green to yellow. Soon, they will be boldly red.

The day is gentle, soft. A breeze is playing with yellowing autumn leaves - the sun is dodging clouds. After walking along the lane, sun-dappled with moving shadow, I am now sitting on the grassy cliff-top looking across the sea. It is still, shining silver, a million splintered sunbeams dancing on its surface. It is 'all sky' - soft, silver touched, palest blue drifting grey. Seagulls are calling to each other, their cries echoing across the water. Grass-hoppers chirrup around my feet, yet stay hidden in the grass - the air smells of wood-smoke. This is a special place, its subtle water colour blues, greys and greens so undemanding.

It is now early evening and the sun, reluctantly setting, made me stop to look - leaning on the cottage window sill. Merging into vivid orange, changing to apricot, it rests on a glassy sea. Towards Heald Brow it turns to a softer peach, before settling finally behind the trees. A fittingly spectacular close to an amazing day.

It's a sure sign of approaching Winter - the huge spiders are looking for Winter lodgings. As I opened my door before bedtime, in ran an enormous spider, straight for the cover of an in-accessible corner. I surprised more in the bedroom. Hopefully, they will respect my space, otherwise, I shall evict them to the outhouse.

The only sign which betrayed Autumn this morning was the depth of the sun, and the 'chrysanthemum smell' of the air. A wren sang by my window, the delicate song ending in a flamboyant trill. Blue sky touched green field. It was a fresh morning.

The month is coming to a close - grey, damp and misty. A fitting back-cloth to the amber russet of Autumn. The greylag geese flew noisily over my cottage. They have decided it is time to leave, so now, only the resident flock at Leighton Moss remain.

September's last day, and after a rainy start, sun shone, lighting the fields to a clear sparkling green. The sea became a dazzling mirror - breezes tugged at clinging leaves, releasing the tired ones to blow about the garden.

October

For the first week of October I have been in a warmer clime, so waking up today to a shining white frosty world was surprising, and so lovely. The garden has gone back to nature in my absence, and all the woodland trees have decided they are ready to release their tired leaves. It's funny how excited I am to see the Autumn leaves, and how disheartened I feel when they lie faded and sodden on the ground! My son is busy sawing up logs for the fire, so out I go, gloves, wheelbarrow and rake to clear the leaves and stack them for next year's leaf mould.

Now is the time for capricious winds. Large wet leaves flew frantically about - commuters in the rush hour. An abandoned umbrella flapped dejectedly in the road looking like an injured bird.

After yesterday's rain and winds, today was still and clear. Seaweed made a lace curtain on the wire fence at Jenny Brown's Point. It had been draped and deserted by yesterday's high tide. I picked 8lbs. of mushrooms - and inadvertently disturbed a conversation between the heron and two swans. The heron rose slowly, swooping over me, away to find solitude.

A RIOT OF THORN AND LEAF

My walk with the dog today over Heald Brow was such a contrast to yesterday. Sitting on the Brow to look at my cottage across the fields, I felt such peace and pleasure. Flies buzzed lazily around my head, Red Admiral butterflies settled on remaining flowers. An Indian summer indeed.

These are my favourite walks, pushing feet through golden leaves, rustling, releasing smells of wet vegetation mixed with wood-smoke. Foraging through chestnut leaves to find spiky shells, break them open and discover shining brown conkers lying snug in their soft green bed.

Today began with a flaming sky. The mellow sun tempted dog, cats and me into the garden. Wandering into the wood, I could hear scratching, rustling. Toads in the garden have gone now to where the compost sits. Clearing the leaves means carefully raking to avoid them.

Over-night, a crop of fungi has appeared on the grass - a miniature village. The rustic steps have also grown a curious crop of fungi. It juts out in weird futuristic shapes. Dainty cobwebs trim the hedge and reach out mysteriously across the path. They cling to my face as I walk through them.

The marrow and ginger jam was still warm, lined up in neat golden rows. It seemed the time for a walk. Sun the colour of ripe apples filtered through the archway of leaves across the lane, turning the path into a golden river. Autumn wore her red beads of bryony - trailed her amber gown. Red Admirals rested on Michaelmas daisies. It was a timeless day with a sense of waiting - stillness. Birch trees silver-trunked, golden leaved, larches wearing last year's dress - the smell of nutmeg and spices. My walk today took me through a farm at Arnside Tower. Farm cats weaved in and out of my legs, purring. Hares chased across the field.

The month progresses; high tides have flooded up to the Dyke. Greylags flew upwards in noisy confusion, disturbed by the dog. She ran through large shining pools of water, splintering sun spangles into fragmented sun-beams. A bull bawled in the distance, birds called across the silvery space. Into the wood, nearly bare branches reached to touch each other. The last leaves fluttered down like snow-flakes to settle on the path. I could hear a church bell from St. Johns in Silverdale echoing across the fields.

As always, I began to tidy my Autumn garden, became distracted by greylags flying over-head - and downed tools. Grey clouds moved across the sky - gold-edged. As I walked along the stream, a heron rose silently in front of me to soar, silhouetted against grey clouds. Like me, maybe he feels free within the bounds of his life, loving the solitude - the loud silences. He reached into the arms of the wind, flew to the melody of the incoming tide.

Gales have come suddenly, tearing the last leaves from branches, making them dance in frantic spirals. Now, they lay exhausted, lining the wet lanes with a carpet of green and yellow.

Winds of 80mph tear at the cottage, hurling huge raindrops at the windows. The yellow bryony leaves which looked so elegant in the hedges, now cling in a desperate bedraggled state. Three cats sit in a disgruntled row on the window sill. They are not impressed at all.

Autumn sun has high-lighted cobwebs, which decorate the cottage window. They cling tenaciously despite a strong breeze trying hard to dislodge them. So fragile, fine threads woven and spun into lace. Deceivingly fragile, they tremble, yet stay in place. No point in sweeping up leaves today, as the breeze takes great pleasure in scattering all my neat piles. The two smallest cats think this is a game I have invented just for them. Diving, playing hide and seek - what the wind doesn't scatter, the cats do.

Just when Autumn's dress begins to look shabby and the evenings early dark, the setting sun becomes a spectacular burst of colour. Looking from my cottage window, I watch the sky in ever changing bands of purple, lilac, salmon pink, peach, then into indigo, as night quietly approaches. The ever-changing kaleidoscope reflecting in a sea now turned to liquid gold.

An Autumn day - still and mellow. Wood smoke curling slowly upwards, mingling with the smell of fallen leaves and chrysanthemums. No breeze today, so its back to the wheel-barrow and the leaves again. It is these tired waiting days that stay in the memory throughout long Winter months.

I 'stole' a walk to Jenny Brown's Point today, when I should have been doing other things, but the day was so still, my walk took precedence over jobs. The trees on Heald Brow were on fire, leaves like amber flames flickering. Leaves lay on grass and rocks, paper-dry, rustling underfoot. No one about, so I ran, kicking leaves to hear them crackle. Sitting on the grey limestone rocks, the empty sands stretched before me, sweeping curved channels, still water-filled, waiting for the incoming tide. The cry of a curlew echoed into the silence. Scrambling over rocks is a special pleasure, and arriving at Wolf House Gallery to a log fire and hot coffee is a lovely way to get breath back before walking home over Heald Brow. Standing at the top of the Brow, I could see my cottage sitting at the foot of the Crag, and I wished I was a crow. Just a few minutes flight across the field, and home!

To Haweswater this morning, and the early sky is clouded palest peach, veiling the morning sun, reflecting in the lake. Amber-gold leaves still cling to trees, reflecting in the water, flooding it into liquid gold. Cobweb mist still lifting from the water's surface gave the lake a mysterious feel.

The breeze wraps me around in the smell of ripe apples. I look across to the random pools left by a receding tide. The lane is strewn with leaves, lying in wet profusion, and slippery to walk on. Secret whisperings in the trees as a soft breeze breathes its Autumn message - 'Soon I will be stronger. Then - I will strip the paling leaves from your branches'. The now bitter blackberries still sit on their rambling brambles - not even desired by birds now. Deep orange afternoon sun looking almost edible was somehow solid in its density of colour.

Driving back home along the wet road, we met a crisis today. We were brought to a halt on the M6 slip road to Carnforth by a swan, half grown, waddling in sad confusion in the fast lane. Her cygnet-grey feathers still growing amongst the white, though she was full size. We picked her up, neck first, and struggled down the slippery steep bank to the canal. Feeling happier, we drove on, only to see another half grown swan waddling clumsily on the slip road. Cars were hurtling past at alarming speeds. Yet again, we carried out the rescue, this time having to carry the swan much further to the canal. I wondered if on their first flight, they had mistaken the wet road for water. The day ended in true style with a sudden alarming commotion in the cat garden. Three terrified cats shot into the cottage - fur in a ridge, tails spread wide. Lux sat at the cat flap swearing, while great big Cobweb and Daisy hid behind chairs. The cause of the panic was a black cat who had managed to find a way into the garden, but couldn't get out again. After a chase which ended in the kitchen, we succeeded in rescuing him and calming him down before letting him out. It was some time before my cats settled down again.

Dense grey rain clouds cling to the hills this morning, and I walk through thick cloying mist, like cobwebs in a long forgotten room.

Midnight at Crag Foot: it was a Gibbous moon - the silence, breathless and expectant. Pale silver-blue light gave the fields an eerie clarity, trees making stark silhouettes against the blue-black sky. Moonlight, a searching luminosity, in contrast to the mellow sunshine of the Autumn afternoon. Gone now the glowing amber, replaced by cool frosty moon-shine. No warmth now as she looked earthwards. Her glances now cold in their searching. Leaves, frost-stiffened, crunched beneath my feet breaking loudly into the stillness. A cow called - the mournful sound echoing, an intrusion into the cathedral reverence of the night. I paused, watched my breath released onto the night air - spiralling in a mist before me. Rabbits ran nervously into hedges. The moon's searching light making them easy prey for hungry foxes. Owls hooted their questions as they swooped over-head making dark shadows across the moon's face. If I held my breath, would this hush last for ever? If I breathed out, would the silence shatter like breaking glass? Cobwebs caught in an instant in the spotlight moonbeam, tremble - lacy fragility giving no hint of strength. This is the kingdom of the moon, where she reigns in solitary haughty splendour. No place for me here, I am an intruder in the world of the night, where cats become primeval, shrews and rabbits hide, and the countryside lies in homage to the ethereal moon.

This afternoon I have walked in the woods watching a mellow Autumn sun turn the paths into gold. I have walked ankle deep in fallen leaves, watched squirrels chase through the branches, and stood for a timeless moment watching a damsel fly who honoured me by resting on my hand. What a lovely way to say farewell to October.

November

I awoke to sunshine - its gentle fingers crept across frosted fields, touching the cottages at Jenny Brown's Point, stretching outwards towards Leighton Moss, edging bracken russet gold. There are so many days like this, when the sheer beauty of where I live fills me with wonder. I walked through lanes from the cottage garden. Pheasants ran across my path making a fuss. The frost of the previous night which had transformed the fields, now melted in the morning sun.

At tea time today, routine chores came to a halt. Rain across the sun, and a magnificent double rainbow spanned the fields. It reached across the sky, its brilliant colours stark against sullen grey clouds. Trees on Heald Brow became illuminated in a multicoloured spotlight.

The first real frost; A fairy-tale picture of white fields, silver leaves. Early sun stretched and woke, reaching over the Moss to the fields beyond. Bracken still lay frost white where the sun's fingers had yet to touch. Lapwings wove silver patterns in the sky, rising high before falling in long sweeping curves.

Days become darker, and now, I am thinking of long evenings by my log fire, curtains drawn against the cold and gales. Today though, there

NOVEMBER

is still colour and life in the year. Swollen grey-black clouds burst open to shafts of sun - spotlighting the fields. Two swans, strong wings beating in unison, flew over-head. I watched them disappear, white against the dark sky.

Although the day began with sunshine, fog soon wrapped a blanket across the countryside. Greylags landed in the field - very noisily as always. Fog had now turned to mist, muffling the sound of their arguments. By four-o-clock mist had rested on the fields like old dusty cobwebs. Curlews' calls penetrated through the stillness. All seemed to be waiting, maybe for Winter. Trees clutched their last few yellow leaves, not wanting to let go. Invisible cobwebs trailed across my face as I walked homeward through the darkening wood. One dog in front of the fire, all cats fed and washing contentedly on chairs and window-sill - and on the kitchen heater. I settled down, content until the morning.

The morning was warm and still, mist, now gone. Through Eaves wood I passed a large group of bird watchers, so there must be a special bird about. Though I have listened to all views, shooting still bothers me. I passed people carrying guns, and wondered about the confrontation between the first group and the second. Because the day was warm and inviting, I walked on to the Bird Reserve. Silver feather-like reed grasses on the Moss made a sibilant whispering sound as they bent to the gentle winds across the fields. Back home again, kettle on, and the robin staring in at me through the window as he clung to the rough stone wall. This was my reminder to fill up the bird table. If the nut hopper becomes empty, the blue tits and various finches knock their beaks on my window to jog my memory.

Lapwings in the frosted field with the sheep on a bright clear morning. I walked along the top Crag Road towards the village. Silvery fields and rooftops of Warton looked ghostly and unreal, as the village appeared out of the mist which was still lying over low ground. Sun melted the remaining veils - smoke from early morning fires spiralled upwards into the sun's light.

Four thirty on a November evening, and the light changes scenery yet again. Dusk arriving reluctantly - the sinking sun bathing fields and trees in a translucent grey-peach tinted glow. Pearly mist rising from the sea floated slowly inland, merging into the peach sky.

The dull grey damp days have arrived, brightened this morning by the woodpecker breakfasting from nuts hanging outside my window. I have had to use a metal hopper to make sure there are still some for the other birds. Woodpecker was very annoyed yesterday - hammering his beak against the mesh. Today, he has his own bag, which he tears large holes in! Still, the fallen nuts feed other birds. The hoppers are an endless spectacle for my kitten, who watches them closely from the cottage window-sill.

Another rainbow today - arched from one field to another. Perfect in its curve, it was a brilliant shining bridge against a leaden November sky. The foot of the bow lit a corner of the field, suspending for a moment, an autumnal bush in its spotlight of iridescent colour.

Midnight on a wet lane - I stood still, staring into the unblinking eyes of a barn owl. After a very long moment, he lifted effortlessly into the black night, and was gone. Far more important things on his mind than my wonder.

The Autumn winds are blowing the last leaves from the trees. Damp November mists rotting them into the ground for next year's re-birth. All things in nature have their purpose and reason. Each thing with its place, its time, and its reason for being.

November, and the grass lies dejectedly beneath its covering of faded leaves. Fog hangs over sea and fields, damp and grey. It muffles the sounds of cockerels crowing. Moisture drops hang in a row on the fence waiting for an unsuspecting passer-by. The wood has become sparse, all her leaves now shed. Bare tree trunks look sinister, their twisted trunks veiled in fog. The grey mood has affected the cats. No frisking this morning - just tentative sniffs and carefully placed paws, shaken at intervals to remove the wet, clinging leaves.

The musky smell of wood fires and wet autumn leaves, a damp afternoon with fading colour - so, I set to in the garden, cutting down the dead vegetation. I have all the herbs I need already dried and put into jars and lavender bags, so lavender, fennel and tansy all had a hair-cut. Such a nostalgic scent of lavender and aniseed mingled together. Twisted spirals of grey smoke rose slowly into the air, hovering above me. It gives the cats a new game as they chase leaves, the smoke trails, my fingers, and each other.

Sun today made false promises, so warm and soft. Despite the month, birds sang loudly. A single robin in a bare tree, trilled happily as I raked up leaves lying sodden on the grass. Not only the birds seemed fooled by a sun reluctant to go, but daffodils have already pushed optimistic shoots through the grass.

NOVEMBER

Tonight, I walked along the lane, over the Crag into Warton. The night was black and still. Walking in the dark is a fascinating experience - so much more to sense and to feel. Stars studded the night sky, dark tree shapes became dancing figures, primitive men, monsters. Shadows moved, swirled - creating strange illusions. I stood silent to watch a small deer wander in front of me - bats circled, owls hooted. Standing on the Crag top, Warton lay below me, a twinkling golden fairy landscape resting at the Crag's foot. Village lights shone for a second time, reflecting in the flooded fields.

A frosty night followed by a day so sharp and clear. Fields have been lightly dusted with silver, and the ground is hard beneath my feet. Daffodils poking through the lawn prematurely are now regretting their hurry. The birds are having trouble in finding food, so tap on my window demanding help. Putting out nuts and bird seed cakes to their urgent requests, I watched the greylag geese flying in ragged formation towards the RSPB Reserve. They stay all Winter, our permanent residents, allowing the visiting geese to fly away without them. The flock seems bigger this year, and their daily comings and goings give me both pleasure and amusement. These clear frosty days seem to have animated the cats, who charge from garden to cottage chasing each other like kittens. Beau, my very old dog, watches enviously, longing to join in the fun. It's a case of spirit being willing though the flesh is weak!

This evening, just before dusk, the sound of rushing wind drew me outside. A peach-gold sky was sinking into a peach-gold sea. The smiling half moon sat just above bare trees, seeming to sit on their branches. Then, the rushing sound again, as wave upon wave of starlings flew over-head on their way to roost. The sky became black with starlings, their wings beating together in a symphony of sound. This nightly miracle fills me with wonder - each time anew.

The countryside had stayed frost-white all day. This morning, green patches left on the field where sheep had lain overnight. Now, in the early evening, the whiteness settled like an enveloping blanket. This is an evening for log fires, drawn curtains and buttered crumpets.

This month has been so warm and wet. Fields and lanes are flooded. Leaves, reluctant to go, cling on to branches still. The ones that have fallen are causing my paths to be treacherous.

Trees and plants are confused! Buds on branches and flowers on polyanthus - both thinking it's Spring before we have had Winter.

A RIOT OF THORN AND LEAF

Now, suddenly, a few cold days with morning frost, have taken me by surprise. The cat flap, long since without its cover to prevent cats trapping their paws, is letting in an icy draught. A duffel bag drawn up over the hole seemed perfect. Hearing a commotion in the kitchen, I investigated. Three cats stood with eyes popping, watching a duffel bag running across the floor. A fourth cat, annoyed and embarrassed, emerged from the bag, turned her back, and washed. I'll have to re-think the draught!

December

Novvember has merged silently into December, and grey mist clings to the countryside like a shroud. Trees, not seeming to mind, huddle together in resignation, naked branches entwined for comfort. Greylag geese fly over-head - a noisy discordant, loveable rabble. Lapwings feed in the field opposite my cottage. Walking by the stream, I surprised the heron, who rose majestically, swooping low over the fields, reflecting in mirror pools left behind by an ebbing tide.

A RIOT OF THORN AND LEAF

Grey mist has become grey rain; three small kittens who live next door, have come in to lie by my fire, oblivious to the crackling and spitting of the logs. Nicely warm, their attentions turn to the dish of conkers on the table. Tabitha expertly flips them out with her paw, Marmaduke and Motley chase them. My cats continue to sleep, only betraying awareness with the occasional flick of an ear. The damp and wet weather has sent spiders scurrying into the cottage. Living so close to the wood, it's the very big hairy-legged variety that visit. As long as they keep to their chosen corners, we can all live in harmony, but I draw the line at my bedroom. Tonight, an enormous spider ran from my covers! Off I went for the glass tumbler and cardboard - my patent spider catcher. I have become expert at the quick painless removal of my guests - putting them into the outhouse to 'winter'.

The greyness had gone this morning, and a transformation had taken place. It was a white, still world; powdered fields, frosted ice trees - silver spangled. A pheasant made a splash of russet against the whiteness. One apricot rose remained, now crystal edged. Curled amber leaves, crisp-sparkled, glistened in the winter sun. How I love this place, with its many moods and faces - now become a new wonderland of ice. Lapwings rose, shining white in the sun's light, falling again, drifting like snowflakes across the early morning field.

Hills lay this morning like an unmade bed beneath a white satin quilt. Brown earth ruts in the fields, now frozen, were filled with snow. Powdery light, it drifted softly. Trees held snow drifts in the curve of their branches. Mid afternoon, and a pale blue-washed sky brushed with soft grey and apricot, melted onto the hills casting magical shadows of moving light. Beech leaves curled russet brown around my feet, frosted silver. The stream raced over stones, carrying sunlight on its surface.

A walk today in Cringlebarrow woods - the fields and trees iced and decorated for Christmas. A silent wood lay sleeping beneath the carpet of dulled copper leaves, now crystal-edged. Enormous limestone boulders, moss covered, stood as they had for centuries, tongue ferns peeping out from their crevices, deeply green against the copper and white woodland floor. A soft-eyed donkey came to nuzzle into my hand - so appropriate for December.

Strong winds are blowing from the sea today, and a great spotted woodpecker is clinging tenaciously to a bag of nuts put out for the blue tits. He has stayed for ages, testing out the bird stand as well! Other birds have patiently waited for their turn, the robin sits on the bird table waiting for his crumbs.

The wind has gone, as suddenly as it came. It doesn't fool me though, I know it is only lurking somewhere, gathering its forces for another onslaught.

Blue tits peer into my sitting room and tap the window with their beaks as the nuts have all gone again. A robin clings to the wall and stares at me because the bird table is empty. So, its outside again to replenish supplies. The haunting cries of lapwings echoes through the stillness, and geese fly to their feeding places, noisy and disorganised as usual. All is well in my world.

Just as I thought! - gales are blowing again, 80 miles per hour, bringing rain. These are the days I love to go to Jack Scout cliffs, cling on to the railings, and watch white horses racing to the shore. The winds pull at my limbs, and deafen me with their roar, and I feel exhilarated. The gales are destructive - mindless hooligans tearing down trees - and the rustic arches in my garden. A bunch of fresh red roses was laid on the cliff-top. It's sad to think of someone being unhappy in such a lovely place.

Over the past few days, mild weather with rain and strong winds have been the pattern. The few dry sunny days in between have been my opportunity to do final garden tidying.

Primroses flourish, bulbs peer through dead leaves, the sun is warm and the birds are singing. Yet Christmas is just three weeks away! Weathermen say it's the mildest winter since 1600 and something.

This afternoon I went into the naked wood to find a dead branch for my Christmas tree. The trees make dark silhouettes against a silver sky. I still find that walking without Beau, my Labrador who is no longer with me, just isn't the same. I miss her such a lot. A deer ran before me, startled by the crack of dried twigs underfoot.

The damp weather has not been without its problems. Black paw prints over my clean covers have been a mystery, as they wouldn't wash out. This morning, the mystery was solved, as Daisy Mae, my white cat, emerged from the coal bunker! I have now, very firmly, blocked it off.

Winds have howled around the cottage all day. They have hurled stabbing spikes of sleet against the windows - whined beneath the door - coaxed and cajoled down the chimney, causing smoke to fill the room. Now the electricity cables are down, and we are without light etc., The cake in the oven will be flat, but it's all a wonderful adventure! Candles are burning in the hearth, and potatoes are roasting in the flames.

The wind blew all night; sucking in his giant breaths with angry gulps, blowing it out in violent howling bursts. It screamed 'let me in' at the closed doors - pleaded for admittance at the windows. This morning, anger spent, the wind became a weary sigh. I viewed his devastation: Ragged clouds were forming into peach-grey order, pools of shining water lay still and exhausted over the fields. Along the lane, tree branches were scattered in hurried confusion, and abandoned.

Walking early this morning, the sky a sullen grey, became suddenly darker as starlings flew overhead in a rush of wings. The lake which again lay where the field was, rippled in the wind.

These are the long days before Christmas. Dark days which never seem to become light. The skies have been heavy all day, spilling grey rain from grey clouds. Fields and lanes are now streams and pools. The still countryside lies sodden and resigned.

It has rained all night yet again. I looked across to Jenny Brown's Point this morning through a curtain of raindrops which clung resolutely to my window-pane. The huge lake which was once a field, has become even bigger, joining up with adjacent fields. A narrow band of green, the railway line, then grey sea. I feel as if I am in Noah's Ark! Many water birds have quickly made use of the new expanse of water. Sunshine and a strong wind at lunch-time have dried things up a little, sending infinite ripples dancing across the surface of the 'lake'.

Bare trees make feather shapes, their nakedness outlined against the sky. Rain has turned to sleet, so it is good to go into the cottage and dry off by a log fire.

Christmas not too far away now, and I have found a small dead branch, sprayed it white, and trimmed it with silver fruit, silver birds, butterflies, and crystal beads. It is my 'magic' Christmas tree, sparkling in a corner of the sitting room. The freezer is full, the logs are stacked, so now I can anticipate the 25th with pleasure. Parcels are mounting up around my branch, and inside the cottage, we are warm and cosy. My object for the next few days is to protect the branch from curious cats.

Still the mild weather persists. The only difference being, that there is now rain as well. There were a few half-hearted gales, not up to Crag Foot standards, but now, it's just grey, monotonous rain. Golden leaves have turned into soggy heaps, and I have a cottage full of bored cats chasing each other to pass the time.

DECEMBER

Cobweb sits by the cat flap (which is now permanently open to allow his huge bulk to squeeze through!), and stares vacantly. So far, he has been there for an hour, willing the rain to stop.

Four days to Christmas; I stood at my window and watched a cold winter sun mellow into flaming gold. As I stood, it melted into amber, and rested on the sea. Still watching - it became soft grey streaked, and turned into night. Such a gentle ending to a clear frosty day that has left puzzled spring flowers wilted and sodden. I have left frosted foot-prints in the grass. The oncoming night promises to be hard-cold.

Christmas Day, and the sun smiled at her reflection in the flooded field. As her smile touched the surface, it splintered into a myriad sparkling sunbeams. My walk to Haweswater took me through wooded paths, bracken-edged. Russet beech leaves trembled, their hold onto branches, tenuous. Two deer ran out in front of me, but on hearing my footsteps, they melted into the trees. Horses were galloping around the field, tails up, just glad to be alive. Everywhere there is promise. Catkins, still tight shut - buds on trees, just waiting for Spring.

Last day of December, and a walk by a rushing river which burst onto fields, bubbled over rocks, showing clearly the excess of rain. Looking up to the distant hills, their snowy tops seemed a fitting end to the year.

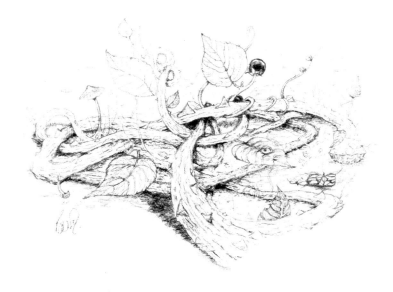

Epilogue

On leaving the cottage – Spring 1999.

The Crag has been there since the beginnings of time. Since the turbulence of the Ice Age, it has rested its jagged grey limestone rocks, covered them with a riot of thorn and leaf, and remained.

Then came Windy Scout Brow wood – curling itself around the foot of the Crag, withstanding gales hurled from the sea, it has flourished. Dense green branches reached out and held each other to hide the woodland paths where violets, primroses, daffodils and orchids bloom happily in Spring. Birds found its haven, calling – building nests. The wren came every year, singing her special song. Foxes hid within its shelter – deer slid silently through dense undergrowth.

Then came the cottage; it nestled at the foot of the Crag, rested itself into the arms of the wood, became a part of it. Over years, the wood reached out protective arms to enfold the cottage, shielding it from sea winds, spreading flowers across the garden. Deer, shrews, toads, moles, foxes visited the cottage. Bats took up residence in its loft. Each creature making it their own. Birds sang their songs, filling each corner of the cottage with magical sound. Sun's fingers reached through its windows, touching crystals to send a myriad rainbows around the rooms.

I became a part of all this. I shared the Crag, the wood, flowers, animals, birds. Each season brought with it special joys. The gales of winter, the mists, the burst of new life in spring. Midnight hours spent watching toads – early mornings spent in awe of darting bats. I marvelled at the unfolding of the year – found security in the predictably unpredictable patterns of the Crag and wood.

Now, I have grown into the cottage, as it in its turn has grown into the wood and the Crag. We have become moulded into each other – there is no distinction between us. Look into the wood, watch it silently enfold the garden, reaching out to touch the cottage. Look even closer, and you will see me. I am there, growing into the tree, blending into the garden, melting into the stone of the cottage walls. We have become inextricably, a part of each other, and a part of me will never leave it.

Other books from Hayloft:

A Country Doctor by Dawn Robertson
(£2.25, ISBN 0 9523282 32)

Military Mountaineering by Retd. Major Bronco Lane
(Hardback, £25.95, ISBN 0 9523282 1 6)
(Paperback, £17.95, ISBN 0 9523282 6 7)

Yows & Cows by Mike Sanderson
(£7.95, ISBN 0 9523282 0 8)

Riding the Stang by Dawn Robertson
(9.99, ISBN 0 9523282 2 4)

Secrets and Legends of Old Westmorland
by Peter Koronka and Dawn Robertson
(Hardback, £17.95, ISBN 0 9523282 4 0)
(Paperback, £11.95, ISBN 0 9523282 9 1)

The Irish Influence by Harold Slight
(£4.95, 0 9523282 5 9)

You can order any of the above books by writing to:
Hayloft Publishing, Great Skerrygill, South Stainmore,
Kirkby Stephen, Cumbria, CA17 4EU.

Please enclose a cheque plus £2 for UK postage & packing.
Tel. (017683) 42300
For more information see: www.hayloft.org.uk